S E R I E S

A life-changing encounter
with God's Word from the books of

2 PETER & JUDE

NAVPRESS
Discipleship Inside Out®

NAVPRESS

Discipleship Inside Out®

NavPress is the publishing ministry of The Navigators, an international Christian organization and leader in personal spiritual development. NavPress is committed to helping people grow spiritually and enjoy lives of meaning and hope through personal and group resources that are biblically rooted, culturally relevant, and highly practical.

For a free catalog go to www.NavPress.com.

ISBN 978-0-89109-994-9

Unless otherwise identified, all Scripture quotations in this publication are taken from the *Holy Bible, New International Version*® (NIV®). Copyright © 1973, 1978, 1984, 2011 by Biblica, Inc.® Used by permission of Zondervan. All rights reserved worldwide. www.zondervan.com. The "NIV" and "New International Version" are trademarks registered in the United States Patent and Trademark Office by Biblica, Inc.®

Printed in the United States of America

20   19   18   17   16   15   14
17   16   15   14   13   12   11

CONTENTS

ACKNOWLEDGMENTS

The LifeChange series has been produced through the coordinated efforts of a team of Navigator Bible study developers and NavPress editorial staff, along with a nationwide network of field-testers.

AUTHOR: DIETRICH GRUEN
SERIES EDITOR: KAREN LEE-THORP

HOW TO USE THIS STUDY

Objectives

Most guides in the LifeChange series of Bible studies cover one book of the Bible. Although the LifeChange guides vary with the books they explore, they share some common goals:

1. To provide you with a firm foundation of understanding and a thirst to return to the book.

2. To teach you by example how to study a book of the Bible without structured guides.

3. To give you all the historical background, word definitions, and explanatory notes you need, so that your only other reference is the Bible.

4. To help you grasp the message of the book as a whole.

5. To teach you how to let God's Word transform you into Christ's image.

Each lesson in this study is designed to take sixty to ninety minutes to complete on your own. The guide is based on the assumption that you are completing one lesson per week, but if time is limited you can do half a lesson per week or whatever amount allows you to be thorough.

Flexibility

LifeChange guides are flexible, allowing you to adjust the quantity and depth of your study to meet your individual needs. The guide offers many optional questions in addition to the regular numbered questions. The optional questions, which appear in the margins of the study pages, include the following:

Optional Application. Nearly all application questions are optional; we hope you will do as many as you can without overcommitting yourself.

For Thought and Discussion. Beginning Bible students should be able to handle these, but even advanced students need to think about them. These questions frequently deal with ethical issues and other biblical principles. They often offer cross-references to spark thought, but the references do not give obvious answers. They are good for group discussions.

For Further Study. These include: (a) cross-references that shed light on a topic the book discusses, and (b) questions that delve deeper into the passage. You can omit them to shorten a lesson without missing a major point of the passage.

If you are meeting in a group, decide together which optional questions to prepare for each lesson, and how much of the lesson you will cover at the next meeting. Normally, the group leader should make this decision, but you might let each member choose his or her own application questions.

As you grow in your walk with God, you will find the LifeChange guide growing with you—a helpful reference on a topic, a continuing challenge for application, a source of questions for many levels of growth.

Overview and details

The study begins with an overview of the books of 2 Peter and Jude. The key to interpretation is context—what is the whole passage or book *about*?—and the key to context is purpose—what is the author's *aim* for the whole work? In lesson 1 you will lay the foundation for your study of 2 Peter by asking yourself, "Why did the author (and God) write the book? What did they want to accomplish? What is the book about?"

In lessons 2 through 7, you will analyze successive passages of 2 Peter and Jude in detail. Thinking about how a paragraph fits into the overall goal of the book will help you to see its purpose. Its purpose will help you see its meaning. Frequently reviewing a chart or outline of the book will enable you to make these connections. In lesson 8, you will look at the book of Jude as a whole.

In lesson 9, you will review 2 Peter and Jude, returning to the big picture to see whether your view of the books has changed after closer study. Review will also strengthen your grasp of major issues and give you an idea of how you have grown from your study.

Kinds of questions

Bible study on your own—without a structured guide—follows a progression. First you observe: What does the passage *say*? Then you interpret: What does the passage *mean*? Lastly you apply: How does this truth *affect* my life?

Some of the "how" and "why" questions will take some creative thinking, even prayer, to answer. Some are opinion questions without clear-cut right answers; these will lend themselves to discussions and side studies.

Don't let your study become an exercise in knowledge alone. Treat the passage as God's Word, and stay in dialogue with Him as you study. Pray,

"Lord, what do You want me to see here?" "Father, why is this true?" "Lord, how does this apply to my life?"

It is important that you write down your answers. The act of writing clarifies your thinking and helps you to remember.

Study aids

A list of reference materials, including a few notes of explanation to help you make good use of them, begins on page 113. This guide is designed to include enough background to let you interpret with just your Bible and the guide. Still, if you want more information on a subject or want to study a book on your own, try the references listed.

Scripture versions

Unless otherwise indicated, the Bible quotations in this guide are from the New International Version of the Bible.

Use any translation you like for study, preferably more than one. A paraphrase such as *The Message* can be helpful for comparison or devotional reading.

Memorizing and meditating

A psalmist wrote, "I have hidden your word in my heart that I might not sin against you" (Psalm 119:11). If you write down a verse or passage that challenges or encourages you and reflect on it often for a week or more, you will find it beginning to affect your motives and actions. We forget quickly what we read once; we remember what we ponder.

When you find a significant verse or passage, you might copy it onto a card to keep with you. Set aside five minutes during each day just to think about what the passage might mean in your life. Recite it over to yourself, exploring its meaning. Then, return to your passage as often as you can during your day, for a brief review. You will soon find it coming to mind spontaneously.

For group study

A group of four to ten people allows the richest discussions, but you can adapt this guide for other sized groups. It will suit a wide range of group types, such as home Bible studies, growth groups, youth groups, and businessmen's studies. Both new and experienced Bible students, and new and mature Christians, will benefit from the guide. You can omit or leave for later years any questions you find too easy or too hard.

The guide is intended to lead a group through one lesson per week. However, feel free to split lessons if you want to discuss them more thoroughly. Or, omit some questions in a lesson if preparation or discussion time is limited. You can always return to this guide for personal study later. You will be able to discuss only a few questions at length, so choose some for discussion and others for background. Make time at each discussion for members to ask about anything they didn't understand.

Each lesson in the guide ends with a section called "For the group." These sections give advice on how to focus a discussion, how you might apply the lesson in your group, how you might shorten a lesson, and so on. The group leader should read each "For the group" at least a week ahead so that he or she can tell the group how to prepare for the next lesson.

Each member should prepare for a meeting by writing answers for all of the background and discussion questions to be covered. If the group decides not to take an hour per week for private preparation, then expect to take at least two meetings per lesson to work through the questions. Application will be very difficult, however, without private thought and prayer.

Two reasons for studying in a group are accountability and support. When each member commits in front of the rest to seek growth in an area of life, you can pray with one another, listen jointly for God's guidance, help one another to resist temptation, assure each other that the other's growth matters to you, use the group to practice spiritual principles, and so on. Pray about one another's commitments and needs at most meetings. Spend the first few minutes of each meeting sharing any results from applications prompted by previous lessons. Then discuss new applications toward the end of the meeting. Follow such sharing with prayer for these and other needs.

If you write down each other's applications and prayer requests, you are more likely to remember to pray for them during the week, ask about them at the next meeting, and notice answered prayers. You might want to get a notebook for prayer requests and discussion notes.

Notes taken during discussion will help you to remember, follow up on ideas, stay on the subject, and clarify a total view of an issue. But don't let note-taking keep you from participating. Some groups choose one member at each meeting to take notes. Then someone copies the notes and distributes them at the next meeting. Rotating these tasks can help include people. Some groups have someone take notes on a large pad of paper or erasable marker board so that everyone can see what has been recorded.

Pages 116–117 list some good sources of counsel for leading group studies.

BACKGROUND
Introduction to 2 Peter and Jude

Map of the Roman Empire

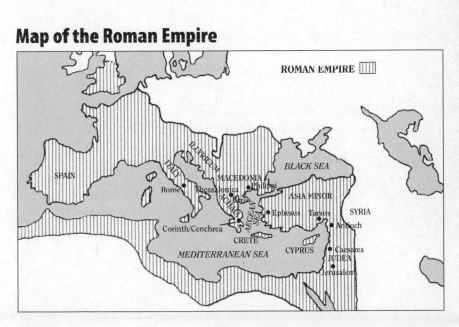

Because of their close relationship, it is expedient, even necessary, to introduce 2 Peter and Jude together because they share so much in common. Both strongly denounce false teachers and apostasy. Both are preoccupied with eschatology (the doctrine of last things), although 2 Peter more so than Jude. Both use peculiar imagery understandable and useful to ancient Jewish Christians, but sometimes opaque to modern readers. These two epistles written to the church at large struggled to gain acceptance into the New Testament, but for different reasons.

Authorship, authenticity, and date of 2 Peter

The author of 2 Peter represents himself as "Simon Peter" and an "apostle" (1:1). His use of the first person underscores a claim to be an eyewitness to the Transfiguration of Christ (see 1:16-18). The author alludes to a previous correspondence with his readership (see 3:1), which many take as a clear reference to 1 Peter. And he refers to Paul as a colleague ("our dear brother," 3:15). Since the apostle Peter was likely martyred at the hands of Roman Emperor Nero (ruled AD 54–68), and if this letter attributed to Peter is authentic, it must have been written sometime prior to AD 68.

However, many scholars doubt that the apostle Peter is the author of the letter bearing his name. They cite many reasons.

- The author had a fluent grasp of Hellenistic Greek which the uneducated fisherman from Galilee did not.
- The letter seems to borrow substantially from Jude, which many believe could not have been written before AD 68.
- The author apparently lived sometime after the first generation of believers ("our ancestors") had passed away (but see note at 2 Peter 3:4, page 75), and when Paul's letters were a collected body of work (but see note at 2 Peter 3:15-16, page 87). These two events had not yet happened by AD 68.
- The author's concern for apostolic tradition and Scripture twisting sound like universal issues of the "late" first century, rather than the local issues of the first-generation early church.
- If the letter was authentic, why did the Roman church take almost three centuries of debate before accepting it into the New Testament canon?[1]

Before we cast aside all such scholarly theories as missing the plain meaning of the text, it should be noted that many works purported to be from the apostle Peter clearly are not, as their content requires a second-century date. A virtual library of pseudo-Petrine literature honors the memory of the chief apostle and trades on his authority: the popular *Apocalypse of Peter* (about AD 135), the widely read *Preaching of Peter* (early second century), the Docetic *Gospel of Peter* (about AD 190), the legendary *Acts of Peter* (second half of second century). These works were alleged sequels or deliberate take-offs of 1 Peter.[2] Still, as some scholars point out, "No other known writing is as much like 1 Peter as 2 Peter."[3]

The difference in style between the literary Greek in 1 Peter (which most scholars agree is authentic) and the rough Greek in 2 Peter may be explained by a change in *amanuensis* (scribe or ghostwriter). The first time around, the uneducated Peter used Silas (see 1 Peter 5:12) as his intermediate agent in writing. For 2 Peter, written just before his death, Peter could have had someone else transcribe his notes who had less command of the language.

The differences in style between 1 Peter and 2 Peter, however significant, may also be accounted for by new subject matter, new format and intent of the letters, new time and occasion of the writing, and new sources or models that he drew upon.

The fact that 2 Peter was finally included in the New Testament canon after such long debate offers more reason to affirm its authenticity. The fact that 2 Peter seems to borrow from Jude does not dictate a late date or another author, but could be an argument for dating Jude earlier than 2 Peter, which softens, expands, and applies Jude's harsh rhetoric.

Second Peter is one of the seven epistles (one to the Hebrews, one from James, two from Peter, and three from John). But the question remains open whether the work is a genuine piece of correspondence with *particular* communities in mind (perhaps directed to the same Jewish Christians scattered throughout Asia Minor, as in 1 Peter). Just as likely, the work could be directed to the church as a whole.

Authorship, authenticity, and date of Jude

Jude had a much easier time being accepted into the New Testament canon of Scriptures than 2 Peter. Yet Jude quotes non canonical sources like the apocryphal *1 Enoch* (see note at Jude 14-15, page 101) and the *Assumption of Moses* (see note at Jude 9, page 98). By freely drawing illustrations from these unapproved sources, Jude was tainted in some theological circles.

Jude ("Judah" in Hebrew or "Judas" in Greek) says he is "the brother of James" (Jude 1). But that still leaves room for speculation, since both names were common in biblical times. *Who's Who in the Bible* identifies seven men by the name of Judas or Jude[4] two were related to a James. Of the two most likely Judas figures, one was an apostle (see Luke 6:16; Acts 1:13)—not Judas Iscariot. But Jude tacitly denies being an apostle (see Jude 17), unlike Peter. The other likely Jude was a brother of Jesus from the household of Joseph and Mary (see Matthew 13:55; Mark 6:3).

However, the author Jude says nothing about a brotherly kinship with Jesus, nor anything about his famous parents—an experience he would have shared with James who was equally silent on this point in his book. Perhaps out of humility and reserve, both authors claim to be no more than "servant[s] of Jesus." Yet the Gospel writers and Paul did not hesitate to make the connection.

As the younger brother of James, who was stoned to death in AD 62 by the Sanhedrin.[5] Jude would have lived a decade or two longer. That means his letter could be dated between AD 70 and 80. But the date of Jude's composition depends upon its relationship to 2 Peter.

If 2 Peter (the longer of the two) is an expansion of Jude for a different audience and occasion—which seems more likely than the other way around—then Jude would have to have been written first, before Peter's death and soon after James's death. A composition date around AD 65 fits all the criteria. And while there are those who believe that "Jude" was a pseudonym and did not compose the letter himself, most scholars agree that "there is nothing in the letter that requires a date beyond the lifetime of Jude the brother of the Lord."[6]

Ancient Gnosticism and its modern-day heretical cousins

The error that both Jude and 2 Peter combat was not the fully developed and systematized form of Gnosticism that prevailed during the second century, but a rudimentary form of Gnosticism plaguing the early church in Paul's day and in John's day.

Because Gnosticism had no central authority or canon of scriptures, its teachers held a bewildering array of views, from asceticism to licentiousness. Common to most views is a dualism that pits God, who is spirit, against the material creation, which is viewed as evil. The human body, comprised of matter, is therefore evil. As a result, there is no resurrection of the body, but, at death, the spirit is believed to travel through space and unite with God. The body was treated most harshly, especially by the ascetic branch of Gnosticism.

An intricate branch of Gnosticism was championed by Valentinus, who came to Rome in AD 140. He propagated a theory of divine emanations and spiritual hierarchies. One of his groups became the so-called *pneumatics*, or spiritual Gnostics, who taught that it didn't matter what you did with your body, leading to deliberate self-indulgence and licentious behavior.[7]

Salvation is understood by Gnostics as an escape from the body, not by faith in Christ or even by good works, but by special or secret "knowledge" (in Greek, *gnosis*, hence "Gnostics"). Christ's humanity was denied in one of two ways. Either Christ only seemed to have a body, a view called Docetism (from the Greek *dokeo*, meaning "to seem"), popularized by the heretic Marcion. Alternately, Christ descended as a dove upon the man Jesus for his adult ministry, from baptism and to Gethsemane, but since only a man could die, Christ on the cross needed a Redeemer too. This view is called Cerinthianism, after its chief second-century spokesman Cerinthus.[8]

Second Peter and Jude were not addressing these intricate, systematic views of Gnosticism, but we can see that some heretical seeds were germinating in the early church and had to be uprooted by Christians taking a stand on apostolic truth.

While both 2 Peter and Jude take a strong stand against early forms of Gnosticism, Peter also takes aim at new errors on the horizon, notably, doubts about the Second Coming and the denial or misuse of authoritative Scripture. These attacks do not come from forces outside the church but from internal factions. Peter also ponders the final cosmic showdown and gives a reasoned explanation for why the catastrophic end of the world is delayed.

The mutual appeal of 2 Peter and Jude is as urgent today as when they were first written. We still need to know truth, as apostasy is more rampant, not only in New Age religions, but also in the amorality of the modern post-Christian age. By basing their case for sanctification on the bedrock of Scripture and the certainty of judgment, 2 Peter and Jude address a question that has divided the Church for two millennia. Historically, Christians have struggled to maintain the proper balance between law and gospel, between discipline and grace. Imbalance toward one produces either a view of complete freedom from the law or legalism and moralism on the other.

Portrait of Simon Peter

Simon was a common name, the Greek version of the Hebrew name *Simeon* (see Acts 15:14). Simon was born in Bethsaida, near the north shore of the sea of Galilee. His family members were Jewish fishermen, like many of their neighbors, although many Samaritans and Greek-speaking Gentiles also lived in Galilee. Simon probably received "the normal elementary education of a Jewish boy in a small town"[9]—that is, he learned to read a little Hebrew and enough Greek to do business, and he spoke Aramaic and common Greek fluently. He was not trained in Jewish Scriptures and law as a rabbi, nor in literary Greek (see Acts 4:13). Before meeting Jesus, Simon may have followed John the Baptist (see John 1:35-42).

Simon was one of Jesus' first and closest disciples. He was always listed first among them (see Matthew 10:2-4; Luke 6:12-16; 9:28; Acts 1:13), and he may have been their leader (see Luke 22:31-32). Jesus renamed him *Cephas* (Aramaic), or *Peter* (Greek), which means a pebble or a small rock. This name suggested Peter's future strength, endurance, and foundational position in the church, and his dependence on the church's true Rock, Jesus (see Matthew 16:16-18; Ephesians 2:19-20; 1 Peter 2:4-8).

Peter seems to have remained the leader of the apostles after Jesus' death (see Acts 1:15-26), although he was leader among equals (see Acts 15:13-22). The first twelve chapters of Acts show Peter leading the disciples' proclamation of the risen Christ. Paul called Peter a "pillar" of the Jerusalem church during this period, from about AD 33–47 (see Galatians 2:9).

Paul and Peter agreed at one point that Paul would evangelize Gentiles and Peter would evangelize Jews (see Galatians 2:7). But Peter did preach to Gentiles in Caesarea (see Acts 10:1–11:18). We don't know what Peter did after AD 47, but 1 Peter suggests that he worked in Asia Minor at some point.

Early sources say that Peter spent the last years of his life in Rome. In AD 64 a fire broke out in Rome, destroying much of the city. Many people suspected that Emperor Nero had ordered the city burned, so that he could rebuild it in a modern style. Nero found scapegoats in an unpopular religious sect—the Christians—who were social outcasts and already suspected of wicked practices. As the Roman historian Tacitus wrote some fifty years later, "a huge crowd was convicted not so much of arson as of hatred of the human race."[10] They were executed horribly.

Although the disgusting executions made many Romans feel sorry for the Christians, the spectacle encouraged others to harass the sect. According to early Christian sources, both Peter and Paul were executed within a few years of the fire in Rome. A third-century Christian, Origen, records that Peter was crucified upside down, feeling unworthy to die as Christ had died.

Relationship between 2 Peter and Jude

Many scholars have noted the close relationship between 2 Peter and Jude, but none more than J. N. D. Kelly, who calls attention to "their startling resemblances in subject-matter, vocabulary and phrasing, and even order of ideas."[11] But a closer inspection of the text will confirm that 2 Peter is secondary and Jude is primary. Kelly notes these similarities and differences,[12] which we can see in the two-column comparison stacking the similar passages side by side:

13

- Jude's style is more spontaneous, vigorous, and harsh.
- The Greek version of 2 Peter is belabored, tedious, toned-down.
- Both catalog examples from biblical history, but while Jude is careless about their chronological order, 2 Peter is very correct.
- While both denounce sin in severe terms, 2 Peter also shows examples of hope, as in the rescue of Noah and Lot.
- In their attitude to Scripture, Jude plays it looser, even quoting from non-canonical sources, whereas Peter deletes these colorful details with his stricter view of the Old Testament canon and his view of an emerging New Testament canon (consisting of Paul's letters).

See for yourself how many points of verbal correspondence—and points of dissimilarity—you can find in the following chart comparing 2 Peter with Jude on page 15.

1. J. N. D. Kelly, *A Commentary on the Epistles of Peter and Jude* (Grand Rapids, MI: Baker, 1981), 235.
2. Kelly, 236.
3. Donald Burdick and John Skilton, "1 & 2 Peter," *The NIV Study Bible*, ed. Kenneth Barker, (Grand Rapids, MI: Zondervan, 1985), 1897.
4. Publications International, Ltd., 1995.
5. Josephus, *Antiquities*, xx. 200.
6. Burdick and Skilton, 1918.
7. E. M. Yamauchi, "Gnosticism," *The New Dictionary of Theology*, vol. 1, ed. Sinclair Ferguson, David Wright, and J. I. Packer (Downers Grove, IL: InterVarsity, 1988), 272–274.
8. Burdick and Skilton, 1906; also Yamauchi, 272.
9. Irving L. Jensen, *1 and 2 Peter* (Chicago: Moody, 1971), 7–8.
10. Tacitus, *Annals*, xv, 44.5 in F. F. Bruce, *New Testament History* (Garden City, NY: Doubleday, 1971), 401.
11. Kelly, 225.
12. Kelly, 227.

Comparative Chart of 2 Peter and Jude

2 Peter	Jude
(1:1) Simon Peter, a servant and apostle of Jesus Christ, To those who through the righteousness of our God and Savior Jesus Christ have received a faith as precious as ours:	(verse 1) Jude, a servant of Jesus Christ and a brother of James, To those who have been called, who are loved in God the Father and kept for Jesus Christ:
(1:2) Grace and peace be yours in abundance through the knowledge of God and of Jesus our Lord.	(verse 2) Mercy, peace and love be yours in abundance.
(1:5) For this very reason, make every effort to add to your faith goodness; and to goodness, knowledge;	(verse 3) Dear friends, although I was very eager to write to you about the salvation we share, I felt compelled to write and urge you to contend for the faith that was once for all entrusted to God's holy people.
(1:12) So I will always remind you of these things, even though you know them and are firmly established in the truth you now have.	(verse 5) Though you already know all this, I want to remind you that the Lord at one time delivered his people out of Egypt, but later destroyed those who did not believe.
(2:1) But there were also false prophets among the people, just as there will be false teachers among you. They will secretly introduce destructive heresies, even denying the sovereign Lord who bought them—bringing swift destruction on themselves. (2:2) Many will follow their depraved conduct and will bring the way of truth into disrepute.	(verse 4) For certain individuals whose condemnation was written about long ago have secretly slipped in among you. They are ungodly people, who pervert the grace of our God into a license for immorality and deny Jesus Christ our only Sovereign and Lord.
(2:3) In their greed these teachers will exploit you with fabricated stories. Their condemnation has long been hanging over them, and their destruction has not been sleeping.	(verse 5) Though you already know all this, I want to remind you that the Lord delivered his people out of Egypt, but later destroyed those who did not believe.

15

2 Peter	Jude
(2:4) For if God did not spare angels when they sinned, but sent them to hell, putting them in chains of darkness to be held for judgment;	(verse 6) And the angels who did not keep their positions of authority but abandoned their proper dwelling—these he has kept in darkness, bound with everlasting chains for judgment on the great Day.
(2:5) if he did not spare the ancient world when he brought the flood on its ungodly people, but protected Noah, a preacher of righteousness, and seven others; (2:6) if he condemned the cities of Sodom and Gomorrah by burning them to ashes, and made them an example of what is going to happen to the ungodly; (2:7) and if he rescued Lot, a righteous man, who was distressed by the depraved conduct of the lawless (2:8) (for that righteous man, living among them day after day, was tormented in his righteous soul by the lawless deeds he saw and heard)— (2:9) if this is so, then the Lord knows how to rescue the godly from trials and to hold the unrighteous for punishment on the day of judgment.	(verse 7) In a similar way, Sodom and Gomorrah and the surrounding towns gave themselves up to sexual immorality and perversion. They serve as an example of those who suffer the punishment of eternal fire.
(2:10) This is especially true of those who follow the corrupt desire of the flesh and despise authority. Bold and arrogant, they are not afraid to heap abuse on celestial beings;	(verse 8) In the very same way, on the strength of their dreams these ungodly people pollute their own bodies, reject authority and heap abuse on celestial beings.
(2:11) yet even angels, although they are stronger and more powerful, do not heap abuse on such beings when bringing judgment on them from the Lord.	(verse 9) But even the archangel Michael, when he was disputing with the devil about the body of Moses, did not himself dare to condemn him for slander but said, "The Lord rebuke you!"

2 Peter

Jude

2 Peter	Jude
(2:12) But these people blaspheme in matters they do not understand. They are like unreasoning animals, creatures of instinct, born only to be caught and destroyed, and like animals they too will perish.	(verse 10) Yet these people slander whatever they do not understand; and the very things they do understand by instinct—as irrational animals do—will destroy them.
(2:13) They will be paid back with harm for the harm they have done. Their idea of pleasure is to carouse in broad daylight. They are blots and blemishes, reveling in their pleasures while they feast with you. (2:14) With eyes full of adultery, they never stop sinning; they seduce the unstable; they are experts in greed—an accursed brood!	(verse 12a) These men are blemishes at your love feasts, eating with you without the slightest qualm—shepherds who feed only themselves.
(2:15) They have left the straight way and wandered off to follow the way of Balaam son of Bezer, who loved the wages of wickedness. (2:16) But he was rebuked for his wrongdoing by a donkey—an animal without speech—who spoke with a human voice and restrained the prophet's madness.	(verse 11) Woe to them! They have taken the way of Cain; they have rushed for profit into Balaam's error; they have been destroyed in Korah's rebellion.
(2:17) These people are springs without water and mists driven by a storm. Blackest darkness is reserved for them.	(verse 12b) They are clouds without rain, blown along by the wind; autumn trees, without fruit and uprooted—twice dead. (verse 13) They are wild waves of the sea, foaming up their shame, wandering stars, for whom blackest darkness has been reserved forever. (verse 14) Enoch, the seventh from Adam, prophesied about them: "See, the Lord is coming with thousands upon thousands of his holy ones (verse 15) to judge everyone, and to convict all of them of all the ungodly acts they have committed in their ungodliness, and of all the defiant words ungodly sinners have spoken against him."

2 Peter

Jude

(2:18) For they mouth empty, boastful words and, by appealing to the lustful desires of the flesh, they entice people who are just escaping from those who live in error.
(2:19) They promise them freedom, while they themselves are slaves of depravity—for "people are slaves to whatever has mastered them."
(2:20) If they have escaped the corruption of the world by knowing our Lord and Savior Jesus Christ and are again entangled in it and are overcome, they are worse off at the end than they were at the beginning.
(2:21) It would have been better for them not to have known the way of righteousness, than to have known it and then to turn their backs on the sacred command that was passed on to them.
(2:22) Of them the proverbs are true: "A dog returns to its vomit," and, "A sow that is washed goes back to her wallowing in the mud."

(verse 16) These people are grumblers and faultfinders; they follow their own evil desires; they boast about themselves and flatter others for their own advantage.

(3:1) Dear friends, this is now my second letter to you. I have written both of them as reminders to stimulate you to wholesome thinking.
(3:2) I want you to recall the words spoken in the past by the holy prophets and the command given by our Lord and Savior through your apostles.

(verse 17) But, dear friends, remember what the apostles of our Lord Jesus Christ foretold.

(3:3) Above all, you must understand that in the last days scoffers will come, scoffing and following their own evil desires.

(verse 18) They said to you, "In the last times there will be scoffers who will follow their own ungodly desires."
(verse 19) These are the people who divide you, who follow mere natural instincts and do not have the Spirit.

---

2 Peter

(3:14) So then, dear friends, since you are looking forward to this, make every effort to be found spotless, blameless and at peace with him.

(3:18) But grow in the grace and knowledge of our Lord and Savior Jesus Christ. To him be glory both now and forever! Amen.

Jude

(verse 24) To him who is able to keep you from stumbling and to present you before his glorious presence without fault and with great joy—

(verse 25) to the only God our Savior be glory, majesty, power and authority, through Jesus Christ our Lord, before all ages, now and forevermore! Amen.

OVERVIEW OF 2 PETER

When a letter from a beloved friend living faraway or nearing death arrives, you read it more than once. The first time through, you read it quickly, looking for general impressions. The second time, you may read it more slowly, taking time to savor each word, perhaps reading it aloud as if to a friend. The third time through, you read more carefully, noting things you want to remember and respond to.

If the letter proved to be the last will and testament of a close friend, you'd keep it for many more readings, reflections, or recitals. This overview study of 2 Peter asks you to read and re-read this brief letter several times, each time with a different purpose or approach.

First impressions

1. Read 2 Peter in one sitting, so you can see the letter as a whole. You may want to read it through again in another translation, or even aloud to get a general impression. What are some examples of the kinds of news Peter shares?

   good news worth shouting about

   _____

   _____

   _____

_____

_____

_____

bad news worth watching out for

_____

_____

_____

_____

news to pray about

_____

_____

_____

_____

2. What other initial reactions or first impulses do you have after reading it?

_____

_____

_____

_____

_____

3. a. What do you notice about the mood of 2 Peter? (Is Peter angry, concerned, joyful, stern . . . ?)

_____

_____

_____

_____

_____

b. Does Peter's mood change in the letter? (Where? Why?)

_____

_____

_____

_____

_____

4. Think about *how* Peter says what he does. How would you describe the *style* or *delivery* of this letter? (Is he helpful, argumentative, personal, encouraging . . . ?)

_____

_____

_____

_____

_____

_____

5. a. Repetition or *how often* an author uses certain words or phrases gives a clue to the author's intent in writing a letter. What words or phrases occur over and over? (Hint: Don't get hung up on the exact wording used, which may vary from translation to translation. Instead go for broad themes. A different version can help you notice new things that make a confusing passage clearer or a familiar passage fresher.)

_____

_____

_____

_____

b. What main themes or topics are suggested by these repeated words?

_____

_____

_____

_____

_____

Broad outline

6. If your impression of 2 Peter is still unclear after reading it twice, a broad outline can help sharpen it. Think of a short sentence or phrase that captures the main point or gives a title to paragraph divisions or other bite-sized Scripture portions. The first one is done for you as an example. (Paragraph divisions, even verse numbers and sentence punctuation, were not in the original Greek or Hebrew manuscripts, but were added centuries later for ease of reading. The divisions in your Bible may differ from the ones given here, so feel free to alter the ones below if necessary.)

    After titling the bite-size portions, cluster them and give an overall title to each chapter or main block of Scripture (1:1-21; 2:1-22; 3:1-18).

1:1-21 _____

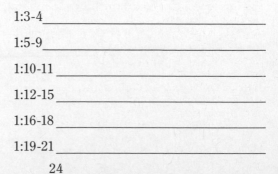

1:1-2 Abundant grace and peace from knowing Jesus

1:3-4_____

1:5-9_____

1:10-11_____

1:12-15_____

1:16-18_____

1:19-21_____

24

2:1-22 _____

  2:1-3 _____

  2:4-6 _____

  2:7-9 _____

  2:10-12 _____

  2:13-16 _____

  2:17-22 _____

3:1-18 _____

  3:1-2 _____

  3:3-7 _____

  3:8-10 _____

  3:11-13 _____

  3:14-16 _____

  3:17-18 _____

After doing this outline procedure on your own, compare your sentence summaries or titles with each other and with the outline on pages 29–30. There is no single correct answer, so discuss in your group why you prefer one sentence summary over another.

Study Skill—Outlining

Outlining a passage will sharpen your focus and increase your retention of the main points. Outlining also helps us understand the flow or train of thought in the book. If it appears some points are subordinate to others, or if some points are mere particulars in relation to a larger general point, you can indicate that in your outline by using capital letters or Roman numerals for main points, and letters or numbers for secondary points.

An outline of 2 Peter might begin like this:

(continued on page 26)

(continued from page 25)
I. Provisions for a fruitful and holy Christian life (1:1-21)
   A. Through the knowledge of Jesus (1:3)
      1. Necessary for life and godliness
   B. Through His promises (1:4)
      1. We participate in God's nature
      2. We escape the world's corruption
   C. Through our moral virtues we "possess" (1:5-9)
      1. [any supporting detail you want to include]
      2. [another supporting detail]
   D. [the main idea of 1:10-11]
      1.
      2.
      . . .
II. [the main idea of 2:1-22]

7. Drawing from your own first impressions and outline summaries, what do you think was Peter's main purpose for writing this second letter? (See 1:12-15; 2:1-2; 3:1-4,8,14,16-18.)

_____

_____

_____

_____

_____

_____

Study Skill—Rhetorical Devices
People usually write letters or address an audience with a particular purpose in mind or some result they want to accomplish in the lives of their readers or listeners. Sometimes writers or speakers underscore their purpose by addressing their audience with a "reminder," with a rhetorical question or statement ("Verily, verily, I say unto you"), or with some other rhetorical device that says, in effect, "This is it. Don't miss this point."

8. If you have not already done so, read the historical background of this study guide. How did the
introductory material get you to rethink some
of your presumptions about the text?

_____

_____

_____

_____

_____

_____

9. In your initial readings of 2 Peter, you may have
come across concepts you'd like clarified or
questions you'd like answered as you go deeper
into this study. Jot down your questions here
to serve as personal objectives for your study.
(Some of your questions may be answered later
in this study guide. The resources listed in the
Study Aids on pages 113–117 may help you
answer the tougher questions.)

_____

_____

_____

_____

_____

Your response

10. What does your group have in common with
the original readers and hearers of 2 Peter?
(Note: Readers today might have a different purpose for studying the letter than the author had
in addressing his original readers.)

_____

_____

_____

_____

_____

_____

11. What could God be telling you and your group to
do in the next several weeks through this letter?

_____

_____

_____

_____

_____

For the group

The beginning of a new group study is a good time to
lay a proper foundation for honest sharing of personal
goals and concerns, as well as insights from your
Bible study. One way to establish common ground is
to share what each group member hopes to get out
of this study of 2 Peter. As you take several minutes
to share each other's hopes and expectations, have
someone write them down. Weeks from now, you can
look back at these goals to see if they are being met.

Take turns sharing some of what you wrote
down from your first impressions (questions 1–5).
Sharing from your notes will help members get
comfortable with each other and establish common
ground for your study.

Likewise, take several minutes sharing your
sentence summaries or titles (question 6), as well as
any comparisons and insights gained from looking
at the chart in the background section. Don't try to
harmonize all your answers, but discuss your differences. Learn why you prefer one sentence summary
over another.

Consider the occasion or purpose of this letter (question 7). What difficult concepts would the
original readers and hearers of 2 Peter have readily

understood, but that you will need more time and in-depth study to understand (questions 9–10)? Take your last ten minutes to share concerns. This input will affect how your group should pace future studies.

Share and pray about how your group will blend your different strengths and backgrounds. Some of you will have strong analytic skills, while others will be good at facilitating group discussion, or driving home a point of application. Give thanks for how God has put your group together, and be willing to help each other. Don't be embarrassed to give and request help. That's why you're studying this as a group, and not just as individuals.

How you divide the time spent in individual and group study will vary according to the group size and purpose, your familiarity with Bible study methods, the willingness of group members to do homework, and the "Optional Application" and "For Further Study" sections. The number of weeks you want to spend on the overall study will also guide your decision of how to pace yourself.

A good rule of thumb for this opening overview study is to allot twenty minutes for individual study and note-taking, then regroup for twenty minutes of sharing your first impressions and outline summaries. The remainder of your hour can be spent reviewing individual expectations and setting group goals.

This timeline assumes you assigned the "How to Use This Study" and the "Background" material as homework prior to this group session. If not, you will need another twenty minutes to review that.

Outline of 2 Peter

Purpose: To encourage believers to live holy lives as they wait for Christ's return.

1:1-21	Peter Describes Ingredients for Christian Growth
1:1-2	Peter identifies with Christ and greets fellow believers
1:3-4	Peter acknowledges that God provides for believers to know Him and live holy lives
1:5-9	Peter encourages readers to practice virtues

2 PETER 1:1-11; JUDE 3

A Fruitful Life

Sometimes it's easy to forget that God has provided us with everything we need for life, as Peter writes in 1:3. Instead we focus on what we think we lack.

Ask God to show you all He has provided you for a fruitful life in Him as you begin this lesson.

God's nature and promises (1:1-4, Jude 3)

1. How does the author identify himself to his readers (see 2 Peter 1:1, see also 1 Peter 1:1)?

   SERVANT & APOSTLE

   _____

   _____

   _____

   _____

   _____

Servant (1:1). The Greek word used in this verse has two meanings: a "slave"—one bought with no freedom to leave, or a "bondservant"—one

For Further Study:
Peter states that Jesus is both God and Savior (see 1:1). For other verses that ascribe deity to Jesus, see Matthew 1:23; 28:19; Luke 1:35; 5:20-21; John 1:1,3,10,14,18; 5:18; Romans 1:4; 9:5; 2 Corinthians 13:14; Philippians 2:6; Colossians 1:15-20; 2:9; Titus 2:13; Hebrews 1:3,8; Revelation 1:13-18; 22:13.

who chooses to serve his master out of loyalty or indebtedness.

Apostle (1:1). Literally, "one who is sent"—a messenger, diplomatic representative, or ambassador. In Jewish law, this person was fully authorized to act or speak on behalf of another. The early church reserved this title for those men who had seen the risen Jesus and gave them the highest authority.[1]

Study Skill—Seeing the Big Picture

When a doctrinal teaching ("Jesus is God") is found in one verse of Scripture, it is important to confirm that teaching with other clear instances in the Bible. We must look at the big picture, reading each verse in terms of its chapter, book, and the whole Bible. For example, when we search the Scriptures to see who else ascribed deity to Jesus, we find that the four Gospel writers, Paul, and the authors of Hebrews and Revelation did.

---

2. What have the recipients of this letter been given (see 1:1-4; Jude 3)?

GIFT OF FAITH

VALUABLE

& FREE

GRACE & PEACE

Faith (1:1). This term is capable of two interpretations: (1) a body of truth handed down by the apostles and held in common by believers everywhere, as in 1 Timothy 4:6 and Jude 3; or (2) the act of believing or trusting Christ for salvation, as in 2 Peter 1:5. Faith is a God-given capacity that is ours through His justice and His favor.

32

Grace (1:2). God's favor—free, unmerited, and abundant—toward sinful humanity. Here the word refers to the enabling and sanctifying grace the believer uses to live out the Christian life.

Peace (1:2). The Hebrew word, *shalom*, connotes total well-being, an inner rest of spirit in harmony with God. Peace is a gift and, in the New Testament, is also fruit of the salvation Christ gives us through the Cross (see Galatians 5:22).

Knowledge (1:2-3). The Greek word, *epignosis*, is key to the Christian faith as well as heretical Gnosticism. For Christians, this *gnosis* refers to the personal, saving knowledge of Jesus Christ as Savior and Lord. To the Gnostics, this knowledge was something esoteric or philosophical, often kept secret. Knowledge is a key word and dominant theme of 2 Peter. True knowledge is always the best antidote to any heresy or apostasy.[2] (See also 1:5-6,8.)

Everything we need for life and godliness (1:3). Peter insists that apostolic truth is adequate for spiritual growth. No secret knowledge, extra blessing, or special revelation is needed, as claimed by Gnosticism.[3]

Study Skill—Observation

When you study the Bible without a study guide, your first step is to make observations and write them down. A good tool for observing everything that is going on in the passage—even things that seem trivial—is to use the so-called W questions—Who? What? When? Where? Why?—and How? You will find examples of those questions throughout this study guide.

---

3. What best describes the gift(s) given to the recipients of 2 Peter:

   a. Is the gift costly or free? (At whose expense?)

   _____

   _____

   _____

33

b. Is it permanent or tentative?

_____

_____

_____

c. Is it for now or for later?

_____

_____

_____

d. Is it for super saints or for needy sinners?

_____

_____

_____

e. Is it universally available, or is it limited in its scope and application?

_____

_____

_____

Participate in the divine nature (1:4). We do not become god-like or perfect, but the Holy Spirit takes up residence in our lives, giving us a new Christlike nature—one that dethrones, but does not entirely remove, the old sin-nature. As we follow God, His influence helps determine what we make of our lives.[4]

An all-out effort (1:5-11)

4. Peter lists seven moral qualities in verses 5-8. He tells us to add each one to the next. What does this tell you about how these virtues are related to each other?

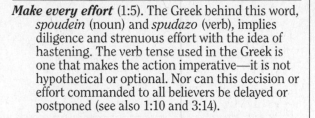

For Further Study:
What is the difference between "knowing" someone and "knowing about" that person? Consider Matthew 7:15-20; Romans 5:1-5; 8:1-17; Galatians 5:1-6; Ephesians 1:3-6; Colossians 1:9-12; James 1:2-8; 2:14-18, and any other cross-references in your Bible.

Make every effort (1:5). The Greek behind this word, *spoudein* (noun) and *spudazo* (verb), implies diligence and strenuous effort with the idea of hastening. The verb tense used in the Greek is one that makes the action imperative—it is not hypothetical or optional. Nor can this decision or effort commanded to all believers be delayed or postponed (see also 1:10 and 3:14).

Add (1:5). The Greek word *epichoregein* (literally, "to supply in addition") originally meant the lavish generosity of some wealthy patron or even the generosity of a husband providing for his wife. The term later came to imply anyone going to great effort at a cost. This verb links all seven of the virtues listed in 1:5-8.[5]

Self-control (1:6). To false teachers of Christian liberty, self-control was completely unnecessary. But to Peter, true Christian knowledge produces a life of self-control springing from a desire to please God.

Mutual affection (1:7). The Greek word *philadelphia* connotes affection, goodness, or virtue in action, directed toward fellow believers.

Love (1:7). *Agape* connotes the universal, self-sacrificing (see John 15:13), "feed my sheep" (John 21:17), and forgive "seventy-seven times" (Matthew 18:22) kind of love that "covers over a multitude of sins" (1 Peter 4:8).

Ineffective and unproductive (1:8). The first Greek word, *argos* (barren or sterile) results in the second, *akarpos* (idleness or sloth), which is the result of not knowing God. Knowing God is effective and produces a life of virtue.

For Thought and Discussion: What happens if believers fail to obey Peter's command to "make every effort"? Is the reward really worth the effort?

For Thought and Discussion: If sanctification is by grace alone, what good are our efforts? Should we continue our efforts or not? Why?

5. Sanctification is the process by which we become more like Christ. What do we learn about the process from 1:5-9?

   a. Is it passive and restful, depending more on God's grace and less on human effort, or does it require effort on our part?

   _____

   _____

   _____

   _____

   b. Do we work on our weakest moral virtue until we gain mastery or is it a continuous process with no one virtue standing out above the rest?

   _____

   _____

   _____

   _____

   c. Is it moral progression, getting better with "increasing measure," or must sanctification be understood in either/or terms—either you have it or you don't?

   _____

   _____

   _____

   _____

Study Skill—"If . . . Then" Clauses

Often the word *if* implies doubt or speculation, but Peter uses it to both encourage and warn his readers. Using "if . . . then" clauses, Peter spells out the consequences of specific actions.

As you study the Bible, keep an eye out for other "if . . . then" statements designed to show us the consequences of certain choices or actions.

6. Peter uses two "if . . . then" clauses in 1:8-9. What are the two possible situations we might find ourselves in?

If _____

_____

_____

then _____

_____

_____

but if _____

_____

_____

then _____

_____

_____

7. What is Peter warning us to do or not do?

_____

_____

_____

_____

_____

_____

Optional Application: Which of the "ifs" in 1:8-9 best describes you? What do you want to do about that?

Study Skill—Cross-References
Parallel or similar passages of Scripture, called cross-references, often shed light on what you are studying. Peter himself makes a cross-reference to Paul and "the other Scriptures" (2 Peter 3:15-16). In this study of 2 Peter, cross-references to 1 Peter, Jude, and to Old Testament allusions will be helpful.

8. a. What does Peter challenge his readers to be or
      to do in light of God's promises and provision
      (see 1:10-11)?

      _____

      _____

      _____

      _____

   b. If God has supplied "everything we need,"
      why is anything more necessary?

      _____

      _____

      _____

      _____

      _____

      _____

Make every effort (1:10).

Calling and election (1:10). When God chooses us
   it is for obedience and godliness.

Eternal kingdom (1:11). Eternal life and abiding
   fellowship with God who is our King.

Your response

9. a. What moral virtue or godly trait do you want to add to your faith this week?

_____

_____

_____

_____

b. How will you do that?

_____

_____

_____

_____

Optional Application: What appetite does having or possessing a God-nature give you? (Is your appetite out-of-control or out-of-character for one who knows God?)

Study Skill—Application

The process of application is guided by the Holy Spirit and by others who have a flair for asking pointed questions to drive home a point. Once a truth or principle is discovered, look for illustrations or ways to apply that truth to your life. Be open to God's leading as you examine your heart and He prompts you to make a decision or take action. Keep in mind that it is better to obey one simple truth of Scripture than to come up with several applications but no plan of action.

---

10. What does participating in the divine nature make you want to do or become? (Are your ambitions in line with someone who knows God's will and purpose? Or have you grown weary of well-doing?)

_____

_____

_____

_____

Optional Application: Who could you gather around you to help bring out the God-nature within you? In turn, who can you encourage to grow in their Christ-likeness?

For Thought and Discussion: Are you sure of your salvation? That is, do you "know" God, or do you only "know about" God?

Optional Application: What steps will you take to persevere in your faith and make sure your election in Christ is one you never lose (see 1:10-11)?

11. How does belonging to and participating in God's nature affect the company you keep and the ways you treat others?

_____

_____

_____

_____

_____

_____

12. Do you have any questions from your study of 1:5-11? Write them below.

_____

_____

_____

_____

_____

_____

For the group

Warm-up. For openers, think about career aspirations, special interests, or heroes you had as a teenager. Pick one of these optional questions:

1. What did you want to be when you grew up?
2. How have you grown in your knowledge—intellectually or culturally?
3. Who was your hero? Why?

Study. For a one-hour study, read 2 Peter 1:1-11 and work your way through the questions on your own. Take twenty to twenty-five minutes for this. Then spend another twenty to twenty-five minutes discussing your answers as a group. This will be the typical time allotment for future group sessions. However, if you have ninety minutes at your disposal, or if you choose to do the individual study as homework before coming to the group, you can take longer discussing questions in the group.

Sharing. For your sharing and follow-up, consider this: While we can't see the wind, we can see its effects. In the same way, we cannot see if a professing believer possesses true knowledge of our God and Savior Jesus Christ. However, we can see moral virtues in action, resulting from knowing God and being empowered by Him. Over time, and with the help of other believers, you can see—and help others see—what qualities you possess in abundance or are increasing in their effect. Take some time to encourage each other in this way.

1. Erich von Eicken and Helgo Lindner, "Apostle," *The New International Dictionary of New Testament Theology*, vol. 1, ed. Colin Brown, (Grand Rapids, MI: Zondervan, 1975), 128.
2. J. N. D. Kelly, *A Commentary on the Epistles of Peter and Jude* (Grand Rapids, MI: Baker, 1981), 298–299.
3. Donald Burdick and John Skilton, "1 & 2 Peter," *The NIV Study Bible*, ed. Kenneth Barker (Grand Rapids, MI: Zondervan, 1985), 1899.
4. Kay Arthur, "Seven Qualities You Can't Do Without," taped lecture on 2 Peter (Chattanooga, TN: Precept Ministries, 1994).
5. Richard DeHaan, *Studies in Second Peter* (Wheaton, IL: Victor Books, 1977), 23.

2 PETER 1:12-21

Eyewitnesses and Prophets

As believers we are heirs of God's kingdom and partake in His divine nature. After showing his readers that God has provided them with everything they need to grow spiritually, Peter reminds them about the Lord Jesus and Scripture. He assures us that we can put our confidence in Christ and know the truth.

A reminder of truth (1:12-15)

1. Peter gives his readers constant "reminders" in 1:12-15.

   a. Of what? _____

   _____

   _____

   _____

   _____

   b. Why? _____

   _____

   _____

   _____

   _____

Remind . . . memory . . . remember (1:12-13,15).
To recall a truth or an event in such a way that
personal choices are shaped by it. A call on God
to "remember" His justice or mercy is a call to
action—there is no suggestion that God somehow forgot.[1] So too with the believers Peter is
addressing.

Know . . . understand (1:12,14,20). The same Greek
word *ginosko* lies behind these two words and
connotes a way of organizing your perceptions
in order to grasp the true nature of something.
To Greeks living before the first century, knowing came through the senses and reason. But in
New Testament times, the Greeks became more
mystical, secretive, introspective, and pseudo-
philosophical. Peter held to the Old Testament
view that knowledge came from a personal
encounter with God.

Tent of this body (1:13). This metaphor, drawn from
a temporary and vulnerable place to live, portrays
the temporary and frail nature of human life,
which is about to end for Peter. This transitory
dwelling stands in contrast to the "rich welcome"
and "eternal kingdom" (1:11) awaiting him.

Christ has made clear to me (1:14). Scripture records
at least one other occasion (see John 21:18-19)
when Peter received clear word of his death, but
that was almost four decades earlier and dealt with
the manner, not the timing, of Peter's death.

Make every effort (1:15). See also 1:10; 3:14. This
verb *spoudazein*, is one of Peter's favorites and
suggests zealous concentration and diligence
that totally energizes the believer, even as he or
she depends on God.[2]

These things (1:15). Peter promises that, after his
death, his readers will have something permanent to remember him by. Various theories have
been proposed as to what "these things" might
be: (a) a future work yet to be composed by Peter
himself; (b) the Gospel written by Mark, who
was with Peter in "Babylon" (Rome) for a while
(see 1 Peter 5:13); (c) the epistle in hand, that is
2 Peter, or (d) some larger body of apostolic tradition—the repository of "the faith."

Optional Application: What truth do you know, but still need to be reminded of?

Optional Application: How can we refresh our memories and remember the truths that Peter discusses?

2. Some of Peter's readers may have said, "We've heard it all before!" or "Tell me something I don't know!" How do you think Peter might have responded to their criticism?

_____

_____

_____

_____

3. Peter conveys truth with deep conviction in the face of pervasive heresy. What is the basis for Peter's confidence, despite facing imminent death?

_____

_____

_____

_____

_____

A confident hope in Christ (1:16-18)

4. How does Peter's relationship and experience with Jesus give him added credibility or authority (see 1:16-18)?

_____

_____

45

_____

_____

_____

_____

5. Jesus asked Peter (and every would-be disciple) "Who do you say I am?" (Mark 8:29). Read 2 Peter 1 again and make a list of everything Peter says about Jesus in this opening chapter.

_____

_____

_____

_____

_____

_____

Cleverly devised stories (1:16). A euphemism for heresies. The Greek word, *muthoi*, refers to fables about gods, creation myths, miraculous happenings, and philosophical speculations of the Gnostic teachers. These fables and speculations stood in contrast to the truthful ("eyewitness") accounts taught by the apostles (see 1 Timothy 1:4; 4:7; 2 Timothy 4:4; Titus 1:14), which only confirmed what the inspired prophets foretold long ago.[3] These popular "stories" cast doubt on the Incarnation and the Second Coming.

6. How can you tell the difference between truth and error? (Do you consider the source? The fruit of their lives? The accuracy of their predictions? Some objective criteria? See also 2:1,10-16.)

_____

_____

_____

_____

For Further Study:
What did Peter experience of Jesus at the Mount of Transfiguration (see Matthew 16:28–17:8; Mark 9:2-13; Luke 9:28-36)?

_____

_____

_____

Coming of our Lord Jesus (1:16). In this context, the Greek word *parousia* refers to Jesus' first coming (the Incarnation), but anticipates the risen Lord (either at the resurrection or the Second Coming; see 3:4,12). This appearance of Jesus in majesty that Peter refers to was likely on the Mount of Transfiguration. *Lord* refers to an honored one or superior, a master, or a sovereign ruler. Jesus is "our" Lord, not in the possessive sense that anyone has a claim on Him, but in the relational sense that Peter and his readers knew this Jesus personally as their superior, master, and ruler.

Majestic Glory . . . sacred mountain (1:17-18). The Mount of Transfiguration, where Jesus was seen in all His supernatural glory with Moses and Elijah (see Matthew 16:28–17:8; Mark 9:2-13; Luke 9:28-36).

For Thought and Discussion: How can we respond to those skeptics who assert that the Bible itself is not much more than "cleverly invented stories"? If asked to "prove" the reliability of Scripture, what would you say?

A firm basis for faith (1:19-21)

7. How is the word of the prophets like a "light shining in a dark place" (1:19)?

_____

_____

_____

_____

_____

8. How did the prophets know what to prophesy?

_____

_____

For Further Study: Are the Apocryphal books, such as the *Assumption of Moses* and *1 Enoch*, to be viewed as "cleverly invented stories," or as the inspired Word of God, when portions of them are quoted in the Bible (see Jude 9,14-15)? Why?

For Thought and Discussion: With all the different religions and philosophies that exist—each with its own prophets and scriptures—how can Christians claim to be right?

_____

_____

_____

Prophets (1:20). Biblical prophecy involved both
forth telling (calling forth godly character
and God-honoring choices) and *foretell-
ing* (predicting future events or interpreting
current events from God's point of view).
More than 300 predictions about Christ were
fulfilled in the Incarnation and His earthly
ministry, and many more point to the Second
Coming.[4]

Completely reliable (1:19). Peter affirms the
reliability and adequacy of Old Testament
prophecy, even in light of events like the
Transfiguration.

Until the day dawns (1:19). Christ will come again
in glory, power, and judgment. This will be a
"shining light" or "morning star" embraced as
a day of salvation by the believer, but dreaded
as a day of judgment by the nonbeliever.

Morning star (1:19). The Greek word, *phosphoros*
(literally, "light-bearer"), refers to Christ, as
some Old Testament prophecies foretold (see
Numbers 24:17; Luke 1:78; Revelation 2:28;
22:16).[5]

**No prophecy . . . by the prophet's own
interpretation** (1:20). This statement is also
capable of two interpretations. According to
one view, all prophetic and apostolic statements are based on historic revelation given
to believers down through the ages. By this
view, no prophecy is privately or independently
interpreted. Rather, the church, aided by the
Holy Spirit and Scripture itself, is necessary
to confirm prophecy. According to a second
view, the verse in question speaks to the divine
origin of prophecy and the apostolic message,
not its interpretation by others. That is, in no
way is prophecy or the apostle's message the
product of a fertile imagination or mere human
interpretation of events. The latter interpretation is supported by the explanatory "for"
which follows in verse 21.[6]

48

Carried along by the Holy Spirit (1:21). While God is the source of Scripture, God's Word always came through human words, that is, truth through personality. Both God and man were active participants in the process that involved sixty-six books written by forty authors over a period of two millennia. By the Holy Spirit superintending the whole process of writing Scripture, the product resulted in an infallible and authoritative Word of God.

Understanding Prophecy

Biblical prophecy foretells the gospel events and thus confirms the reliability of Scripture (see 1:19). See for yourself by checking out the following Old Testament references with cross-references to the New Testament, for example:

Isaiah 7:14 with Matthew 1:20-25
Micah 5:2 with Matthew 2:1
Zechariah 9:9 with Matthew 21:1-9
Isaiah 50:6 with Matthew 26:67
Zechariah 11:12-13 or Jeremiah 19:1-13 and
    32:6-9 with Matthew 27:3-10
Isaiah 53:7,12 with Matthew 27:12-14,38
Psalm 22:18 with John 19:23-24

Your response

9. a. When modern-day prophets speak with a confidence like Peter's, how can you know if their confidence is true or false?

_____

_____

_____

_____

_____

_____

_____

b. What would incline you to agree with their teaching? (The other person has more experience? Has "heard from God"? Knows more Bible? What they predict comes true? What they claim can't be verified?)

_____

_____

_____

_____

_____

10. a. What biblical truth have you been neglecting lately?

_____

_____

_____

_____

b. What truth are you willing to bet your life on?

_____

_____

_____

_____

11. What truth will you ask God to remind you of during the next week?

_____

_____

_____

_____

_____

For the group

Warm-up. This study continues to address those who are not "sure" of their salvation by reestablishing three essential elements of the Christian faith: (1) a deep conviction that truth matters; (2) a confident hope in Christ; (3) a firm basis for faith in an era of apostasy.

Ask group members to share briefly about either an "eyewitness to history" experience, or a personal "mountain peak" experience. The latter can be a literal one (climbing Pikes Peak), or it can be a figurative one (a spiritual retreat high, getting to be "king of the hill" at work, or overcoming a particular plateau in personal growth).

Discussion. After your individual study, come together as a group to share and confirm your understandings and biblical insights. This safeguards the objective truth of God's Word by hedging against the tendency of go-at-it-alone Christians (and cult members) to push private interpretations that deviate from orthodox faith and practice.

As conscientious students of the Bible, we are accountable to others for truth we find, and to be open to the Holy Spirit to apply the objective truths of Scripture.

1. Lawrence Richards, "Remember/Memory," *Expository Dictionary of Bible Words* (Grand Rapids, MI: Zondervan, 1985), 520.
2. Richards, "Effort," 242–243.
3. J. N. D. Kelly, *A Commentary on the Epistles of Peter and Jude* (Grand Rapids, MI: Baker, 1981), 316.
4. Richard DeHaan, *Studies in Second Peter* (Wheaton, IL: Victor Books, 1977), 59–61.
5. Kelly, 322; also DeHaan, 58–59.
6. Donald Burdick and John Skilton, "1 & 2 Peter," *The NIV Study Bible*, ed. Kenneth Barker (Grand Rapids, MI: Zondervan, 1985), 1900; also DeHaan, 55–56.

2 PETER 2:1-16; JUDE 4-12

False Prophets and True Believers

Polls indicate that 96 percent of Americans believe in a supreme being or higher power, but only half of those people attend church even once a month. Religion may be popular these days, but sincerity seems to count more than truth with these "believers." They have little confidence that they can know anything beyond their own feelings. When, as true believers in Christ, we claim to know truth and right from wrong, or if we insist on one way to God, we aren't just quaint or old-fashioned—we are now labeled religiously intolerant or politically oppressive.

The apostle Peter and his contemporaries faced a society in a similar crisis of confidence in the traditional views about Christ. In chapter 2 of this letter, Peter targets the false teachers of his day and makes a stand for truth against heresy, providing us with an example of standing up for truth in a relative society.

The dangers of heresy (2:1-3)

1. How can we identify "false prophets" and "false teachers" (2:1-3)?

   _____

   _____

   _____

53

For Thought and Discussion: What is heresy? Can you think of any contemporary examples that the Scriptures clearly denounce and your group can all agree is heresy?

_____

_____

2. a. What do you think was a bigger problem for the early church—the false prophets' heretical views or God's delay in judgment? Why?

_____

_____

_____

_____

_____

b. Which is harder for you? Why?

_____

_____

_____

_____

3. Even though God's judgment may seem slow in coming, what does Peter tell us will happen to the false teachers?

_____

_____

_____

_____

False prophets . . . false teachers (2:1). These could include the following: (1) those who worshiped false gods or idols; (2) those who claimed to receive special revelations from God, but did not; (3) those who wandered away from the truth into an immoral life and led others astray.[1]

54

Destructive heresies (2:1). Presumably Gnosticism, but this could refer to any deviant teaching.

Who bought them (2:1). This figure of speech refers to the ransom that Christ paid as the penalty for all sin (1 Corinthians 6:20; 7:23; Galatians 3:13).

In their greed (2:3). Motivated by money or commercial advantage, as was the prophet Balaam (see 2:15). However, being a "professional" (paid and retained by the king) was not a fail-safe criterion for discerning a false prophet, since Samuel and Isaiah were both professionals and true prophets.[2]

Fabricated stories (2:3; compare Jude 8). Revelation by dreams was an accepted prophetic technique, common to true teachers or prophets, such as Solomon (see 1 Kings 3:5-15) and Daniel, among others (see Deuteronomy 13:1-5). However a direct word from God was superior and authenticated the Lord's prophet (see Numbers 12:6-8; Jeremiah 23:25,32). Peter condemns these "dreamers" for make-believe stories and fanciful revelations that were out of touch with truth and reality.

Destruction has not been sleeping (2:3). False prophets may seem to get away with their deception and exploitation by ruining the righteous and escaping God's judgment, but their doom will surely come, just as it did in Old Testament times (see 2:4-9).

For Further Study:
False teachers deny the Lordship of Christ by scandalous behavior or by teaching false doctrine. For examples of scandalous behavior, see 2:6,10,13-15. For examples of doctrinal error, see Peter's teaching on the Second Coming (see 3:1-10) and the authority of Scripture (see 1:16-21; 3:15-16).

Study Skill—Examples and Stories
General statements in the Bible are often supported with specifics to help us better understand and apply truth. To make his point, in general, that God's judgment is certain and that no one but the righteous can escape God's judgment (see 2 Peter 2:3,9), Peter (following Jude's model) cites three notorious examples from Old Testament history (see 2:4-8). The force of Peter's argument from Old Testament anecdotes may be lost on modern readers. Yet stories of these catastrophes would have had a significant impact on the original readers and hearers, many of whom had a Jewish background and saw themselves accountable before a holy and sovereign God.

Divine mercy (2:4-9)

4. Peter tells the stories of the angels, the Flood, and Sodom and Gomorrah. What is the point of each story?

the angels _____

_____

_____

_____

the Flood_____

_____

_____

_____

Sodom and Gomorrah _____

_____

_____

_____

_____

Angels when they sinned (2:4; Jude 6). This sin could refer to two instances in the Old Testament. In Hebrew, "sons of God" is rendered "angels" in Job 1:6 and 38:7. Accordingly, the first "sons of God" who married the "daughters of men" prior to the Flood (Genesis 6:1-4) were actually fallen angels (or demons). In marrying these women, these angels left heaven ("abandoned their own home," Jude 6), and went after "flesh of another kind" (see note at 2 Peter 2:6; Jude 7). These fallen angels, with their mortal women, populated the earth with powerfully wicked mongrels ("Nephilim," Genesis 6:4), who perpetuated evil worldwide. That grieved God's heart and subjected the ancient world to universal judgment.[3] Others view these fallen angels as Satan's dominions who were involved in the insurrection of Satan described in Isaiah 14 and Ezekiel 28.

Sent them to hell (2:4). The Greek verb here *tartaroo* means "to confine to Tartaros." In classical Greek mythology, Tartaros was where rebellious gods and evil humans were sent for punishment. *Tartaros* is not the usual New Testament word for hell, which is either *Gehenna* (twelve times), meaning "abyss," or *Hades* (eleven times), translated "the grave" or "Sheol" (a transliteration of the Hebrew), which both refer to the temporary abode of the dead who await final judgment.[4] Peter's teaching concurs with Jesus' statement about a place in hell reserved for "the devil and his angels" (Matthew 25:41).

Noah, a preacher of righteousness (2:5). Peter departs from Jude's tradition by mentioning the exceptional Noah (see also 1 Peter 3:20). Considered a "righteous" and "blameless" man who "walked with God" (Genesis 6:9), Noah was famous for his faith and obedience in building the ark that survived the flood of divine judgment.

Seven others (2:5). Noah's wife, three sons and their wives, plus Noah (the eighth) were preserved to repopulate the earth after the Flood (see Genesis 6:10; 7:7; 9:18-19).

Sodom and Gomorrah (2:6; Jude 7). The sexual immorality and perversion by Sodomite men refers to those who lusted after the two angelic beings whom Lot entertained (see Genesis 19:1-11). The Greek words, *heteros sarkos*, rendered "perversion," literally mean "lusted after flesh of a *different* kind," whereas homosexuality is lust after the *same* kind (see Romans 1:24,27). Nonetheless, men having sex with men ("sodomy" or homosexual acts) is likely a snide inference here.[5] Sexual sin was not the only reason Sodom and Gomorrah were destroyed by fire. Evidently, hoarding surplus wealth and contempt for the poor and needy (see Ezekiel 16:49-50) make Sodom and Gomorrah an example of "pride going before a fall."[6]

Lot, a righteous man (2:7). Lot, the town judge, was Abraham's nephew. Yet he is a perverse channel of God's grace, inasmuch as Lot survived God's judgment of the city, but lost half his family. They lost their lives because they discounted Lot's tarnished witness and stayed or looked behind (see Genesis 19:14,26).

Distressed by the depraved conduct . . . tormented . . . by the lawless deeds (2:7-8). Inexplicably, Lot offered his daughters (instead of two angels) to the men of Sodom. Though conscience-stricken over the sinful conditions around him, Lot kept his mouth shut. He chose not to speak out against, or separate himself from, wickedness at Sodom and Gomorrah.

5. Compare 2 Peter 2:4-9 with Jude 5-7. How do Peter and Jude tell these three stories differently?

_____

_____

_____

_____

_____

_____

Study Skill—Parallel Scriptures
Often passages in the Bible are similar enough that it seems one may have copied the other, or both may have drawn from a common source. Comparing the documents side by side helps us see what one author may have in mind by leaving something out, by rearranging the parts, or by inserting something new. This study skill is helpful when studying the Gospels or parallel accounts in 1 and 2 Samuel, 1 and 2 Kings, or 1 and 2 Chronicles.

In this study, we will compare similar passages in 2 Peter and Jude. For example, by examining both passages about Noah and Lot, we learn that they (plus their respective families) were shown God's mercy because of their righteousness; yet their cities; even their whole known world, were destroyed.

6. It often seems that God is selective in His judgments. On what basis do you think He condemns some and saves others?

_____

_____

_____

_____

_____

_____

_____

How to spot a false prophet (2:10-16)

7. From 2 Peter 2:1-16; what evidence do you find that distinguishes a false prophet from a true one?

_____

_____

_____

_____

_____

_____

_____

Carouse in broad daylight . . . while they feast with you (2:13; compare Jude 12). These open "love feasts" may have accompanied the Lord's Supper, and were more blatant than even in the pagan world, which at least had the discretion to do their corrupt practices under the cover of darkness (see 1 Thessalonians 5:7).[7]

Despise authority . . . heap abuse on such beings (2:10-11; Jude 8-9). False prophets deny the authority of others—the authority of Jesus, of Scripture, or, as here, the authority of "celestial

For Thought and Discussion: What does righteousness look like? Do you know anyone righteous?

For Thought and Discussion: What do you really think of people who act or preach like Noah or Peter? Would you be a "scoffer" like the false prophets of Peter's day?

For Thought and Discussion: Do you view radical end-times preachers with disdain—more like crazies or con men, but not as examples of "righteousness"? Why?

For Further Study: Read the story of Sodom and Gomorrah in Genesis 19. Will intercessory prayer, such as Abraham's, work to save our cities? What else does it take to save a city?

For Further Study:
For other examples
of false prophets who
were clearly identi-
fied and denounced
in Old Testament
times, check out the
following: the 450
prophets of Baal (see
1 Kings 18:18-24); the
400 prophets in King
Ahab's court (see
1 Kings 22); and the
many prophets of
"peace . . . when there
is no peace" (Jeremiah
6:12-15; 8:10-12;
Ezekiel 13:10,16; Micah
3:5-6). What was
condemnable about
these false prophets?

beings." These dignitaries could be angels or
church leaders. Since Jude 8-9 proceed from
the general ("celestial beings") to a particular
example—the archangel Michael—we may conclude the "beings" in 2 Peter are likely angels.

Blaspheme in matters they do not understand
(2:12). To blaspheme is to "slander" (Jude 10)
against God or, in Jude's case, "against
whatever they do not understand." Gnostic
heretics claimed to have a secret, esoteric,
hard-to-understand kind of knowledge. Even its
recipients or practitioners did not understand
what they were talking about. This contrasts
with Peter's intent to convey God-knowledge
that his readers could publicly verify and fully
trust (see 1:2,8,12,20 and related notes).

Like unreasoning animals, creatures of instinct
(2:12; Jude 10). The point of the analogy is
ambiguous. "Unreasoning animals" could refer
to brutish, immoral behavior, that is, day-time
carousing (see 2:13) stemming from their
corrupt desires (see 2:10). Or it could refer to
irrational, senseless thinking (as in "irrational
animals," Jude 10).

Eyes full of adultery . . . they seduce the unstable
(2:14). Not only are false prophets sadly self-deluded
about the truth, they boldly seek to seduce recent
converts (see 2:18; 3:16) or anyone else ignorant
of truth and unstable in their convictions.

Way of Balaam . . . the prophet's madness
(2:15-16; compare Jude 11). A pagan diviner
with an international reputation, Balaam son
of Bezer was hired by Balak king of Moab to
curse Israel—the people God had specifically
blessed—at the time when they were advancing
through Canaan (see Numbers 22–24). Balaam
did not necessarily believe in Yahweh ("the
Lord"), but would sell his soul and his services
for money. This professional prophet spoke
outrageous things on behalf of any god, some
of which are preserved in non-biblical sources.[8]
Though he tried to accommodate Balak, the
greedy Balaam was stopped from cursing Israel
by a donkey who sensed an angel blocking his
path. The donkey verbally rebuked his master,
who would have been killed for his apostasy.

8. How are the false prophets of Gnosticism guilty of
Balaam's "madness" (2:16) or "error" (Jude 11)?

_____

_____

_____

_____

_____

_____

Your response

9. a. Should churches leave the judgment of false
prophets to God? Why, or why not?

_____

_____

_____

_____

b. What can you do to expose the error of their
ways?

_____

_____

_____

_____

For Further Study:
Sometimes false
prophets in Old
Testament times were
hard to distinguish
from true prophets.
Read Deuteronomy
13:1-18; 18:14-22;
1 Kings 13:18-22;
22:1-28; Jeremiah
23:9-40; 28; Ezekiel
12:21–14:11; 22:28.
What distinguishing
criteria do these texts
suggest?

For Further Study:
False prophets,
including many
Gnostics, were
denounced not only
by Peter but also by
Paul (see Acts 20:
28-30; Galatians 1:6-9;
Philippians 3:2;
Colossians 2:4,8,16-23;
2 Thessalonians 2:1-4;
1 Timothy 1:3-7; 4:1-7;
2 Timothy 3:1-8), by
John (1 John 2:18-23;
2 John 7-11), and by
Jude (verses 3-4,8,10).

10. Which of the following characteristics of many false teachers have you witnessed?

- Their rhetorical devices (how slick they are; use of "inflated words")
- What they look like (a "brute beast," a mule)
- How they look at us ("with eyes full of adultery," trying to seduce me)
- Their financial appeals (heavy arm-twisting, tearjerker "made up" stories)
- The company they keep (at "love feasts")
- Their spiritual impact (minimizing casualties, manipulating the unstable)
- Their correlation to familiar doctrine ("whatever I believe")

11. Judgment is most certainly coming, but the righteous will survive. How can you make sure you and your family are among the survivors?

_____

_____

_____

_____

_____

For the group

Warm-up. When has God spared you in the face of adversity, judgment, or destruction? (It could be a health crisis, job trouble, or family problems.) Was it because of something you did (your righteousness) or simply because of God's grace?

Discussion. After your individual study, come together as a group to explore the truths and heresies identified by Peter. Guard against fatalism (knowing that God's judgment is certain) and judgmentalism (of certain people you suspect of being false). With one another and God, embrace the hope and mercy of the gospel.

1. Herbert Lockyer Sr., ed., "False Prophets," *Nelson's Illustrated Bible Dictionary* (Nashville: Thomas Nelson, 1986), 374–375.
2. James Motyer, "Prophecy, Prophets," *New Bible Dictionary* (Grand Rapids, MI: Eerdmans, 1962), 1041–1042.
3. Kay Arthur, "Judgment Is Coming, But You Can Survive It!" taped lecture on 2 Peter; also Richard DeHaan, *Studies in Second Peter* (Wheaton, IL: Victor, 1977), 76.
4. Lawrence Richards, "Heaven and Hell," *Expository Dictionary of Bible Words* (Grand Rapids, MI: Zondervan, 1985), 337.
5. J. N. D. Kelly, *A Commentary on the Epistles of Peter and Jude* (Grand Rapids, MI: Baker, 1981), 316; also Arthur.
6. Pete Hammond, ed., *The Word In Life Study Bible*, (Nashville: Thomas Nelson, 1996), 49.
7. Donald Burdick and John Skilton, "1 & 2 Peter," *The NIV Study Bible*, ed. Kenneth Barker (Grand Rapids, MI: Zondervan, 1985), 1901.
8. Ronald Allen and Kenneth Barker, "Numbers," *The NIV Study Bible* (Grand Rapids, MI: Zondervan, 1985), 223.

2 PETER 2:17-22; JUDE 12-16

What Could Be Worse?

According to pollster George Barna, one out of two professing Christians believe that "all good people, whether they consider Jesus Christ to be their Savior or not, will live in heaven after they die." In a day when individualism runs rampant, the community of faith has eroded; no longer do most Christians share certain core beliefs, or fundamentals, in common. Instead of believing there is no God (atheism) or that God is unknowable (agnosticism), we are living in an age with many competing, "equally valid" ideas about God (individualism).

Springs without water (2:17-19)

1. "These people" in 2:17 refers to the false prophets and teachers Peter described in 2:1-16. Jude describes them as "wandering stars" in verse 13. How are these men and their teachings like "springs without water" and "mists driven by a storm"?

   _____

   _____

   _____

   _____

_____

_____

2. What is their effect on others (see 2:18)?

_____

_____

_____

_____

_____

3. a. What is the fate of these men (see 2:17)?

_____

_____

_____

_____

b. Do you see any hope for them, or is their present fate sealed forever? (Compare 2:17 with Jude 13 and 2 Peter 2:4; 3:9.)

_____

_____

_____

_____

Springs without water (2:17; compare Jude 12). Like a mirage in a desert or mists driven by a storm, promising but not delivering water or rain in a drought, these prophets tease but ultimately disappoint and disappear. Their teachings cannot satisfy those who thirst for spiritual truth. Only Jesus Christ, the fountain of living water, can do that.

Blackest darkness (2:17; compare Jude 13). A euphemism for hell, but Peter omits the "forever" clause that Jude includes.

4. How do these men go about deceiving their flock (see 2:18)?

_____

_____

_____

_____

_____

5. What kind of freedom do they promise? (Freedom from what, or to do what?)

_____

_____

_____

_____

_____

_____

They mouth empty, boastful words (2:18; compare Jude 16). Eloquent false prophets speak fine phrases that have no meaning. By their inflated rhetoric they puff themselves up but convey little truth or moral restraint.

They promise them freedom (2:19). Freedom from moral restraint ("we are no longer under law but under grace") is what some "Christian libertarians" in Rome, Corinth, and Galatia taught (see Romans 6:15; 1 Corinthians 6:12-13; Galatians 5:13). Those who profess freedom from the law misrepresent Paul's truth (see 2 Peter 3:16) and practice licentiousness, resulting in bondage to sin.[1]

Depravity (2:19). This English word is used for five different Greek words in the New Testament, but here means "moral corruption," or spiritual death, resulting in final destruction.

Slaves to whatever has mastered them (2:19).
This proverbial maxim stems from the military
practice of enslaving an enemy defeated in
battle and making him a prisoner of war. This
applies with deadly force to those who yield to
sin, surrendering to its mastery.[2]

Caught in the end (2:20-22)

6. a. Who is being warned in 2:20-22? (Are they
victims of heresy, good people who were never
really saved, or people claiming to believe, but
who lead others astray?)

_____

_____

_____

_____

_____

b. What evidence do you find in the text to support your answer?

_____

_____

_____

_____

_____

7. What are the consequences for those who are
"just escaping" (false cults, idolatry, dead ritual,
lustful desires, sinful human nature, the world's
corruption) and are "again entangled in it and
are overcome" (2:18,20)?

_____

_____

_____

_____

8. Why are these people "worse off" than before (see 2:20)?

_____

_____

_____

_____

_____

For Further Discussion:
According to 2 Peter 2:20-22, is it possible to profess Jesus as Lord, walk in the "way of righteousness," and still lose one's salvation?

For Further Study:
Does Peter teach one thing (in 1:10-11 and 2:20-22) and Jesus another (in Matthew 7:21-23; 12:43 45; 13:1-8; John 10:27-28), regarding a believer's profession of faith, one's possession of salvation, and one's eternal security with God?

The corruption of the world (2:20). This echoes the lustful desires of sinful human nature (see 2:18) and the depravity (see 2:19) to which the heretics are still entangled, though at one time they had at least escaped, or made a moral change in lifestyle, by professing Christ as Lord and Savior.

Way of righteousness . . . the sacred command (2:21). Both are terse expressions for Christianity as a whole, which was first called "the way" (Acts 9:2; 18:25; 19:9,23; 22:4; 24:14,22). The Christian message is holy and one we are commanded to follow. "The sacred command that was passed on to them" is also "the faith that was once for all entrusted to God's holy people" (Jude 3).

9. Peter quotes an Old Testament proverb (see Proverbs 26:11) and cites another one popular in the culture of his day. What point is Peter making through these proverbs?

_____

_____

_____

_____

_____

69

For Further Study:
What hope, if any,
does Peter hold out
for those who once
knew the "way of
righteousness," have
since spurned Christ,
and have returned
to their old sinful
lifestyle?

Proverbs are true (2:22). A proverb is a pithy statement, vivid illustration, or wisdom saying, usually in two parts conveying one spiritual truth.
Two truths, one revealed in Scripture (about
the dog) and one discovered in life (about the
sow), coincide to make one essential point
about the folly or shame of refusing the way of
righteousness (eternal life) and returning to
the wages of sin (spiritual death).

Dog (2:22). To orthodox Jews of Peter's day, dogs
were "unclean," fierce and despicable. To be
called a dog is insulting (see 1 Samuel 17:43)
and to call oneself a dog is self-loathing (see
2 Samuel 9:8) or humility (see Matthew 15:27).
Christians were likened to sheep (see John
10:27-28; 1 Peter 2:25), but never to dogs; only
evil-doers were dogs (see Philippians 3:2).[3]

Sow (2:22). This "unclean" animal was also most
despicable to an orthodox Jew. The pitiable pig-
pen of the prodigal son comes to mind (see Luke
15:15-16). But for him there was repentance, restoration, and a participation in the divine nature,
whereas for the sow in this parable, there is no
change of nature (nor for the dog); both remain
and return to what they were in the beginning.

Returns (2:22). This verb may refer to the moral
U-turn of false prophets or to the backsliding ways of their victims. In either event, the
animal (or human) nature has not changed but
the direction has with disastrous results.

Your response

10. Many of us may know young Christians or seek-
ers looking for answers to their questions, but
who do not know their way around the Bible
and could be easily led astray by false doctrine.
In your own words, what is Peter's warning for
those whom you are raising up, discipling, or
witnessing to?

_____

_____

_____

_____

_____

11. Using Peter's criteria, how can you tell whether someone is truly born again and merely having a moral relapse, or whether someone is forever caught in sin until they trust Christ for salvation?

_____

_____

_____

_____

_____

Optional Application: Suppose someone claimed to know the Lord, but then turned away. To now reach that person for Christ, would he or she need reminding, repentance, regeneration, renewal, or removal? Why?

Optional Application: What spiritual impact does living and working among sinful people have upon you?

For the group

Warm-up. Have you known anyone who turned away after claiming to follow Christ? What led that person astray? Has he or she returned to the faith? How?

Discussion. After your individual study, come together as a group to explore the controversial questions of repentance and faith, of salvation and security. Guard against bringing in your favorite theologians or pastors, but stick to the text. Use the study skills learned in previous sessions to settle any disputes.

1. Donald Burdick and John Skilton, "1 & 2 Peter," _The NIV Study Bible_, ed. Kenneth Barker (Grand Rapids, MI: Zondervan, 1985), 1902; also J. N. D. Kelly, _A Commentary on the Epistles of Peter and Jude_ (Grand Rapids, MI: Baker, 1981), 346.
2. Kelly, 347.
3. J. Nieboer, _Practical Exposition of II Peter_ (North East, PA: Our Daily Walk Publishers, 1952), 196.

2 PETER 3:1-10; JUDE 17-19

Certain Judgment

Our society is preoccupied with the future. With one trip to a bookstore or an hour of talk radio, we sense what scholarly and self-styled futurists are saying about megatrends . . . resources running out . . . political conspiracies . . . economic earthquakes, world catastrophes . . . nuclear holocaust . . . doomsday survival . . . even alien-takeover fantasies. And from the pulpit and the street-corner preacher, we also hear anxious and hopeful concerns about the future and the last days.

Then there are those who scoff at all forecasts of judgment. Peter and the church of his day had to contend with scoffers who cast doubt on the Lord's ever returning, judging his creation or redeeming His people.

No end of scoffing (3:1-4)

1. a. Why is Peter writing a second letter (see 3:1)?

_____

_____

_____

_____

b. Of what is he reminding his readers?

_____

_____

_____

_____

Second letter . . . reminders (3:1). This could be a reference to 1 Peter, on the assumption there is enough continuity of subject matter to qualify 2 Peter as a "reminder." It could also be that chapter 3 (no longer dependent on Jude) was once an independent document and therefore a "second" letter, which was later appended to earlier reminders (see 1:12-15) when the Scriptures were collected into the New Testament canon.

Holy prophets . . . your apostles (3:2; compare Jude 17). These two sources of authority are placed on the same plane, which either elevates Peter's status as one of the apostolic group, or it betrays a later age (later than Peter's lifetime) when the apostles were venerated posthumously. Some of these same commentators argue that the equation of Old and New Testament authorities speaks of an emerging canon of Scripture, which did not happen until the second century.[1]

---

2. a. Who are these "scoffers" (3:3)?

_____

_____

_____

_____

_____

b. At what are they scoffing?

_____

_____

Last days (3:3; compare "last times," Jude 18). This expression does not refer to some remote time in the future, but introduces the era immediately following Christ's first coming.[2] We have been in the post-New Testament era for almost two thousand years.

2/4/17

Scoffers (3:3; see Jude 18). The identity of these people is ambiguous: they may be the same false prophets of chapter 2, as some commentators contend.[3] However, the focus of chapter 3 seems fresh, directed to those who discredit the Lord's return. Gnostics of the second century discounted the notion of God's coming judgment and the need for moral accountability. These scoffers Peter is addressing may be "early" Gnostics.

Since our ancestors died (3:4). This ambiguous phrase refers to either (1) the first generation of eyewitness apostles or (2) the "holy prophets" (3:2), that is, the Old Testament patriarchs (as in John 6:31; Romans 9:5; Hebrews 1:1). If the first is correct, then the dating and attribution of this letter to the apostle Peter is suspect. More likely, the first martyrs (Stephen, James, and other parents or relatives) are in view, and Peter is about to die.

Everything goes on as it has (3:4). The skeptics' argument is this: If nothing (meaning the Lord's return) has happened since creation or "since our fathers died," then the status quo prevails and God never will intervene. This argument had some force because rumors existed that Peter would not die until Jesus returned (see John 21:22-23), yet at the time of this book Peter is about to die.

3. a. Can you empathize with the skeptics' argument that nothing ever changes? How?

_____

_____

_____

_____

_____

b. Why should we pay heed to someone preaching about being righteous and getting ready
for God's judgment when "everything goes on
as it has" for hundreds of years?

_____

_____

_____

_____

_____

An end to scoffers (3:5-7)

4. How does Peter answer the skeptics' problem
with the apparent delay in Christ's return (see
3:5-7)?

_____

_____

_____

_____

_____

5. What does the Second Coming have in common with the Flood story (see 3:6-7)?

_____

_____

_____

_____

Water . . . water . . . waters (3:5-6). The Creation
account indicates that the rise of mountains
caused the waters to separate into oceans and
seas and lakes. Distinct from those waters, and
an agent of Creation and the Flood, is the water
in the atmosphere (see Genesis 1:2,6-10).

The world of that time (3:6). This "world" (in
Greek, *cosmos*) may refer to the whole earth or
entire universe, or it may refer to its inhabitants
(as in John 3:16) or to the places where people of
that day lived. In the first instance, this implies
a universal flood, in the second case, the flood
was localized or more limited in scope.

By God's word . . . By the same word (3:5,7).
The "word of God" is not only verbal truth
(spoken to God's people) and propositional
truth (open to verification), capable of "divid-
ing soul and spirit . . . thoughts and attitudes"
(Hebrews 4:12), it is creative and destructive—
in beginning the world and ending it.

***Heavens and earth are reserved for fire . . .
destroyed by fire*** (3:7,10). Annihilating the
whole world by fire, as a biblical concept, is
unique to 2 Peter. Because second-century
Christian apocrypha and pagan sources
contain similar teaching, some scholars
accordingly place 2 Peter in their ranks.[4]
However, questions about a delay in Christ's
coming arose as early as Pentecost and per-
sisted during the time of Paul's ministry (see
2 Thessalonians 2).

Mercy for all believers (3:8-10)

6. a. How does Peter answer the problem, raised
by the faithful, about the apparent delay in
Christ's return (see 3:8-10)?

_____

_____

_____

_____

For Further Study:
What is the role of
water at the time of
Creation (see Genesis
1:2,6-10)? At the time
of the Exodus (see
Exodus 14:21–15:10)?
At the Day of the
Lord ("day of judg-
ment") (see 2 Peter
3:5-7,10-13)?

77

b. How was the forgetfulness of his "dear friends" different than that of the scoffers?

_____

_____

_____

_____

c. How was Peter's response different?

_____

_____

_____

_____

A day is like a thousand years (3:8; compare Psalm 90:4). Peter is unique in using Psalm 90:4 as the interpretative key in explaining the apparent delay in the end times. Eloquent theories about Creation, the messianic age of the church, the Great Tribulation, the millennial reign of saints in judgment, and so on, have been predicated by taking this equation literally every time a biblical timetable is presented.[5]

Study Skill—Noncontradiction

Since all truth is God's truth then there is no contradiction between (1) truth specifically revealed and affirmed by God in Scripture and (2) truth (re)discovered by scientists. Paradoxes do exist, such as why the earth appears old to most geologists if six days (millennia) of creation makes the earth no more than 10,000 years old. Whether or not the Bible supports only a "young earth" theory is beyond the scope of this study. But the law of noncontradiction drives most Bible scholars to believe that the "how" and "when" of Creation is beside the point of biblical accounts, which focus more on the "who" and "why" of Creation.

7. How does the Lord's patience differ from slowness (see 3:9,15)?

_____

_____

_____

_____

_____

Slow . . . slowness (3:9) Literally, "slack," implying impotence or negligence.

Patient (3:9) The word implies forbearance and recalls the days of Noah when God "waited patiently" (1 Peter 3:20). The idea of repentance (see 3:9), or turning around and going the other way, is invariably given as the reason for God's patience.

8. a. What will the "day of the Lord" be like (3:10)?

_____

_____

_____

_____

b. Should we take Peter's prophecy literally? Why, or why not?

_____

_____

_____

_____

Like a thief (3:10). The word implies unexpected suddenness and recalls the teachings of Jesus (see Matthew 24:43; Luke 12:39) and Paul

For Thought and Discussion: It took 120 years for the Flood to happen and many scoffed at Noah's preparations. Now, many scoff at the apparent delay in the Lord's "imminent" return. At what biblical truths have you heard people scoffing? How have you responded?

For Further Study: Throughout the Bible, God's rebellious people are reminded of His forbearance, His great mercies, His slowness to anger. Read Exodus 34:6; Numbers 14:18; Psalm 86:15; Lamentations 3:22-23; Ezekiel 18:23; 33:11; Jonah 4:2; John 3:16; Romans 2:4; 9:22; 1 Timothy 2:4; and 1 Peter 3:20. What stories or principles come to mind as you study each verse in context?

79

(see 1 Thessalonians 5:2). John the Seer also used this imagery (see Revelation 3:3; 16:15).

Heavens disappear with a roar . . . elements will be destroyed by fire (3:10,12). Peter is borrowing apocalyptic (and highly symbolic) language common to Daniel and Revelation. Some believe that Peter had Hiroshima or other nuclear holocausts so feared in the Atomic Age in mind, but lacked the vocabulary to express it. Others believe this end-times language is purely symbolic, and that the first-century was so far removed from the twentieth, that prophesying the atomic bomb is impossible.

The earth and everything done in it (3:10). "Everything" could be physical and chemical elements composing all matter. The term could also refer to human inhabitants and to the works we create (human civilization, moral achievements) that all come before God's judgment. See also note on "world" (3:6).

9. Look at the either/or questions below and compare notes with group members to see if you can achieve any consensus. Discuss your views and try to find support for your answers in Scripture.

   Is the Day of the Lord inevitable, or avoidable?

   _____

   Is there a specific date, or is the timetable open-ended and indefinite?

   _____

   Is it a foregone conclusion, or can it be renegotiated by prayer or good works?

   _____

   Is it "imminent," or is it as far removed from today as today is from Christ's ascension, AD 29?

   _____

Is it universal, or selective in its effects?

_____

Is it a one-time occurrence, or does it manifest itself periodically and repeatedly through history?

_____

Is it brought on by self-destruction, or by a natural catastrophe, or by something supernatural, defying all "laws of nature," as we know them?

_____

Your response

10. Which of the statements below describe your understanding of God's patience?

   ☐ I am persistent in prayer, which gets me in sync with God's timetable.
   ☐ I often run out of time and give up hope. (I hate to "hurry up and wait.")
   ☐ I need reassurance that God's plan is still on time. ("How long, O Lord?")
   ☐ I am grateful because I need time for God's mercy to take effect.
   ☐ I wish God operated on human time.
   ☐ I think God is too patient with certain people.
   ☐ It doesn't concern me because I spend little time thinking about the present heavens and earth being destroyed one day.
   ☐ Other: _____

   _____

11. How have you benefited from the Lord's patience or apparent slowness?

   _____

   _____

   _____

   _____

   _____

   _____

12. How does Peter's perception of God compare to yours? (Is your God "too small"? Or is He "big enough" to create, destroy, and redeem?)

_____

_____

_____

_____

_____

_____

For the group

Warm-up. To begin this session, get the group to focus on what it is like to experience delays or postponements in the fulfillment of a promise.

"What were you once promised as a child or young adult that never materialized"—for example, a fishing trip, a graduation present, a certain privilege, a marriage proposal, a pay raise, "justice"?

"What did you patiently and persistently wait for that eventually came to pass, as promised, and that was all the more appreciated because you had to wait for it?"

Discussion. After your individual study, explore the controversial questions surrounding the Flood, the Second Coming, damnation, and divine providence as a group. Guard against haranguing all the "scoffers" and "ungodly men" you may know. Instead, keep the focus on God's word to you, and be sure to leave enough time to do the response section.

1. J. N. D. Kelly, *A Commentary on the Epistles of Peter and Jude* (Grand Rapids, MI: Baker, 1981), 354.
2. Donald Burdick and John Skilton, "1 & 2 Peter," *The NIV Study Bible*, ed. Kenneth Barker (Grand Rapids, MI: Zondervan, 1985), 1902.
3. Kelly, 355.
4. Kelly, 360–361.
5. Kelly, 362.

2 PETER 3:11-18; JUDE 20-25

Living in the Last Days

For years, nuclear scientists, ecologists, and social scientists have been predicting a catastrophic end to the world as we know it. Conspiracy theorists, cult leaders, science fiction writers, and Pollyanna politicians predict a radical new world order in its place.

The apostle Peter, two thousand years ago, also predicted a disintegrating universe, but he doesn't leave us floating on some cold, abandoned death star called Spaceship Earth. With convincing optimism, he foresees the day after the "day of the Lord" when a new heaven and new earth will be established. Peter's prediction makes all the difference in the world!

What a difference a day makes (3:11-13)

1. The "day of God" (3:12) is a day like no other. How does Peter describe that day?

   _____

   _____

   _____

   _____

For Thought and Discussion: Will the day of the Lord be one climactic event visible to all people at once? Or will the end come at various times throughout history?

2. How is the "day of God" like, or unlike, the "day of the Lord" (see 3:10, and questions 8–9 of lesson 6.)

_____

_____

_____

_____

_____

Since . . . destroyed (3:11). This fiery destruction and disintegration of the heavens and the earth is unique to the New Testament. Knowing that this world will end should make a difference in how we live and relate to others.

Holy and godly lives . . . spotless, blameless and at peace (3:11,14). This life of separation from sin and devotion to God is what makes believers stand out from those who perish in the end.

Day of God (3:12). This unusual expression may be synonymous with the "day of the Lord" (3:10), as it is associated with similar end-time events.[1] Alternately, the day of God could be the eternal state, the new heavenly dwelling, or "home of righteousness"—symbolic of the final triumph of God's people ushered in after the Lord's return and God's judgment has cleaned house. This cosmic finale, according to this view, will cap the 1,000-year reign inaugurated by the Lord's return.[2]

Hastening the Lord's Return

Some believe that mere mortals, no matter how godly, can do nothing to "hasten" the day of the Lord. Yet, we are asked to "look forward to" an event at least 1,000 years away. If there's nothing we can do to hasten that day, we are left wondering why Peter urges his readers to "speed its coming." And if the Lord's return does somehow depend on our godly lifestyle and evangelistic efforts, we have no excuse for waiting around.

3. a. What is holding up the Lord's return (see 3:8-9,12)?

_____

_____

_____

_____

b. What, if anything, would "speed its coming"?

_____

_____

_____

_____

Look forward (3:12). The Greek verb *prosdokontas* is used elsewhere in the New Testament to describe the eager anticipation that greeted certain events that were only hours, even moments, from happening (see Luke 1:21; Acts 3:5; 10:24).

Speed its coming (3:12). The Greek verb *speudontas* implies "hastening," and was misinterpreted during the Crusades to mean that the Millennium, or 1,000-year reign of the saints, could be ushered in by aggressive evangelism and social action. In the Talmud there is a related Jewish teaching that the Messiah would appear if all the Israelites would truly repent and keep all 612 laws for just one day.[3] Compare this with Acts 3:19-21, which seems to imply that repentance and conversion hasten Christ's return.

His promise . . . a new heaven and a new earth (3:13). This image of the cosmic finale is first developed by Isaiah (see Isaiah 65:17; 66:22) and later by John (see Revelation 21:1), who describes this new entity in terms of the New Jerusalem.

Where righteousness dwells (3:13). The ultimate dwelling place of righteousness is the New Jerusalem, which replaces our earthly tent and the Old Jerusalem, even the earth itself, as a place where God dwells in perfect holiness.

4. What promise does Peter give us about the hopeful outcome of the "day of God" (3:13)?

_____

_____

_____

_____

Standing strong in the last days
(3:14-16)

5. How should we live as we anticipate the last days that Peter describes (see 3:14)?

_____

_____

_____

_____

_____

6. How does "our Lord's patience" (3:15) affect the end times?

_____

_____

_____

_____

_____

_____

7. In 3:15-16 Peter mentions Paul and his writings.

a. What did Peter say about Paul?

_____

_____

b. His writings?

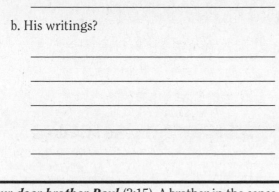

_____

_____

_____

_____

_____

Our dear brother Paul (3:15). A brother in the sense of a fellow apostle, not just a kindred spirit.

Wisdom God gave him (3:15). Peter's endorsement of Paul tacitly confirms that what he wrote was "inspired" writing—the Holy Scripture.

All his letters (3:16). This does not necessarily refer to a collected or complete body of Paul's letters in the New Testament, because the canon of Scripture did not close for decades after Paul and Peter wrote their last letters.

Hard to understand (3:16). It may be that the meaning of Paul's writings was difficult to interpret, but more likely that Paul was dealing with sacred mysteries and great truths of Christianity, which were difficult to fully comprehend.

Distort . . . the other scriptures (3:16). False prophets intentionally twist Scripture to suit their own purposes.

Closing words (3:17-18)

8. a. What are Peter's readers "forewarned" about (3:17)?

_____

_____

For Thought and Discussion: Peter and Paul wrote "the same way" and dealt in like manner with "these matters" (3:16). How has studying 2 Peter helped you understand some of the difficult concepts in Paul?

For Further Study: See what Paul writes about God's patience in Romans 2:4; 3:25; 9:22-23; 11:22-23, and about moral readiness for the Second Coming in Romans 13:11-14; 1 Corinthians 1:7,29-31; 2 Corinthians 5:6-10; Ephesians 4:30-32; Philippians 2:15-16; Colossians 3:4-17; 1 Thessalonians 5:4-11.

b. If they already have this knowledge, why do some of them still fall prey to "the lawless" (3:17)?

_____

_____

_____

_____

You have been forewarned (3:17; compare Jude 3-5). Either Peter did not need to repeat what he said earlier in the letter (see 1:11-15; 3:1-3), or his readers had already received the apostolic faith delivered "once and for all" to all the saints, and knew enough to reject false doctrine.

Error of the lawless (3:17). This refers, in the immediate context, to distorting Scripture (see 3:16). Perhaps the false prophets wanted to start a Paul versus Peter controversy. Or perhaps they introduced a subtle difference in apostolic teaching, just enough to discredit the whole Bible. In either event, they were unprincipled and lacked a firm foundation.

Your secure position (3:17). This does not refer to the eternal secure standing of legal righteousness that believers have in Christ, or the preservation of the saints, but rather to its corollary: the perseverance of the saints. The implication is that believers can grow slack in their steadfastness, and so should grow in grace.

9. Is knowledge enough to keep one's position with God secure (see 3:17)? What else is necessary?

_____

_____

_____

_____

_____

88

Grow in the grace and knowledge (3:18). This benediction reminds us of Peter's conception of Christianity as one of "grace," "growth," and "knowledge" (see 1:3-11 and related notes).

---

10. What is Peter's parting admonition and benediction to his recipients?

_____

_____

_____

_____

_____

_____

11. How does Peter's benediction compare with Jude's (see Jude 24-25)?

_____

_____

_____

_____

_____

_____

Your response

12. Do thoughts about the day of the Lord fill you with joy and expectation, or with dread? Why?

_____

_____

_____

_____

_____

_____

13. What can you do to grow in the grace of the knowledge of God?

_____

_____

_____

_____

_____

Learning the Hard Way

Peter received and grew in grace the hard way— through adversity. After being rebuked by Jesus for being impatient with His timetable and then denying the Cross, Peter was empowered by the Transfiguration of Christ (see Mark 8:31–9:13; 2 Peter 1:16-18). After denying his Lord three times, Peter received forgiveness and a threefold restoration (see Matthew 26:31-35,69-75; John 21:15-17). A third hard lesson in grace came after Peter knew what the gospel was all about, but nonetheless tried to reserve the indispensable grace of God for Jews only. For this failure to discern grace at work in the Gentiles, Peter was rebuked by Paul (see Galatians 2:11-21).

14. Have you experienced hard, but lasting, growth in grace? When?

_____

_____

_____

_____

_____

_____

Optional Application: Are you susceptible to the lure of cults and false prophets, and in danger of "falling" from your secure position in Christ?

15. What questions, if any, do you still have from this lesson?

_____

_____

_____

_____

16. What is one thing you will do this week to obey God's Word to you from 2 Peter?

_____

_____

_____

_____

_____

For the group

Warm-up. Remember that the purpose of these warm-up questions is to introduce group members to each other and to introduce the theme to everyone. For this lesson, get the group to focus on one of two fanciful scenarios: Either ask "If you were in charge of the world's calendar, would you speed it up or slow it down?" Or, ask of their experiences in being creative or destructive: "Which would you rather be in charge of—creating the world in six days or destroying it in one?"

Discussion. After your individual study, come together as a group to explore the questions that lead to a better understanding of the end times. Pay special attention to the response section, especially the summary questions. Close by sharing the one area of growth that each of you is willing to commit to (question 16).

1. Donald Burdick and John Skilton, "1 & 2 Peter," *The NIV Study Bible*, ed. Kenneth Barker (Grand Rapids, MI: Zondervan, 1985), 1903.
2. Richard DeHaan, *Studies in Second Peter* (Wheaton, IL: Victor, 1977), 127–128; William MacDonald, *II Peter & Jude: the Christion and Apostasy*, 57–58; and J. N. D. Kelly, *A Commentary on the Epistles of Peter and Jude* (Grand Rapids, MI: Baker, 1981), 367.
3. Kelly, 367.

JUDE 1-25

Final Results

We conclude our study of 2 Peter and Jude by delving into the book of Jude by itself. Jude is the alleged source for much of what 2 Peter (especially chapter 2) says on the subject of Christians and apostasy.

Read carefully through Jude before beginning this lesson, taking note of its outline. Compare the outline of Jude with the outline of 2 Peter. Note the significant differences in their treatments of the Christian and apostasy. Where Peter raises the prospect of new converts backsliding in faith and denying the Savior, and then refocusing their attention on the Second Coming and the authority of Scripture, Jude paints a much bleaker picture. He sees an apostasy that undermines grace, disdains authority, and appears beyond repentance and redemption. Yet he, too, closes on a note of mercy and the need for perseverance.

Introduction (1-2)

1. How does Jude identify himself (see verse 1)?

_____

_____

_____

_____

For Further Study:
Jude doesn't flaunt his brotherly kinship with Jesus, for he knows that the spiritual connection is the most important. What did Jesus teach about who His real brothers and sisters were (see Matthew 12:48-50; 13:55-56; Luke 11:27-28)?

For Further Study:
What major theme(s) are announced in Jude's greeting (see verses 1-2) and resumed in the benediction (see verses 24-25)?

Brother of James (verse 1). Jude is also the brother of Jesus, one of four other sons of Joseph, but declines to introduce himself that way (see introduction, page 9).

2. To whom was this letter written?

_____

_____

_____

_____

_____

_____

3. How does Jude characterize the relationship of his readers to Jesus?

_____

_____

_____

_____

_____

Called (verse 1). This Greek adjective, *kletos*, functions like a noun and came to be equated with "a Christian," as all Christians had a vivid sense of God's call on their lives (see Romans 1:6-7; 8:28; 1 Corinthians 1:24; Revelation 17:14; see also 2 Peter 1:10 and related note on page 38).

Loved . . . love (verses 1-2). The Greek word *agape* also lies behind *dear friends* (literally, "loved ones"; Jude 3,17,20).

Kept (verse 1). The job of keeping or preserving the saints from falling belongs to God (see Colossians 1:17; Hebrews 1:3).

Exposing the apostasy (3-4)

4. a. What kind of letter did Jude want to write (see verse 3)?

_____

_____

_____

_____

b. Why did he change his mind?

_____

_____

_____

_____

For Thought and Discussion: What would Jude say to those cult leaders who say their books are equal in authority with Scripture? What would he say to those who have something new to add to Scripture?

Contend (verse 3). This word implies a wrestling match or some other contest of wills and Olympic strength. There's nothing specifically Christian about this word, as many Greek writers used this athletic image to describe their battles.

The faith . . . once for all entrusted to God's holy people (verse 3). This faith is not a verb, as in the act of believing in Christ for salvation, but a noun form of faith, that is, the body of truth or belief system considered orthodox, finished, complete, and "most holy" (verse 20) by the Church.

---

5. a. Who are these men that Jude is warning his readers against (see verse 4)?

_____

_____

_____

_____

For Thought and Discussion: How can we guard against those who would secretly slip in among us and stir up trouble?

For Thought and Discussion: How do people today change the grace of God?

b. Why do his readers need to be warned?

_____

_____

_____

Certain individuals (verse 4). Exactly who these men were is unknown to us, but they were presumably known to the readers—although not at first, as they "secretly slipped in among" the Christians.

Whose condemnation was written about long ago (verse 4). The reference may be general, either in the Old Testament or by the apostles (see verses 17-18), or in Enoch's prophecy (see verses 14-15). Or it could be specific and divine judgment, recorded in some heavenly books, that has yet to happen, but (by human reckoning) is long over-due, which is the sense of 2 Peter 2:3.[1]

Pervert the grace of our God into a license for immorality (verse 4). Exchanging the freedom of grace *from* sin for the freedom *to* sin is based on one of two fallacies: (1) God will forgive by His grace all sins we commit with impunity, or (2) all our sins magnify the grace of God, so let sin abound. Both views are apostasy. Paul spoke about this reasoning to the church, which feared that justification by faith might lead to moral irresponsibility (see Romans 3:8; 5:20; 6:1,15; Galatians 5:13).

Deny . . . our only Sovereign and Lord (verse 4; compare 2 Peter 2:1). The Greek construction of this statement indicates that "power without limit" or "absolute dominion" is applied to a single person, Jesus, who is both Sovereign and Lord.[2] For a similar point, see 2 Peter 1:1 and related note.

A lesson from history (5-11)

6. Peter uses Old Testament examples to make his point clear. What do these "ungodly people" (verse 4) have in common with . . .

96

the unbelieving Israelites (see Numbers 13:26–14:35)?

_____

_____

_____

_____

the fallen angels (see Genesis 6:2,4; Matthew 25:41; 2 Peter 2:4)?

_____

_____

_____

_____

the Sodomites (see Genesis 19:15; 2 Peter 2:10)?

_____

_____

_____

For Thought and Discussion: Is damnation something God chooses for "certain people," or is it just the consequences of our actions? How does Jude support your view?

Destroyed those who did not believe (verse 5). The Israelites who failed to believe Joshua's and Caleb's report of the Promised Land (see Numbers 13–14; 1 Corinthians 10:5-10) were condemned to wander the desert for forty years without entering into the Promised Land.

The great Day (verse 6). The end, or final judgment, as in Acts 2:20 and Revelation 6:17.

Sodom and Gomorrah and the surrounding towns (verse 7). Of the five Cities of the Plain, only one (Zoar) escaped judgment (see Genesis 13:12; 18:16–19:29). See notes on 2 Peter 2:6 (page 57).

Punishment of eternal fire (verse 7). This refers to hell. The "burning sulfur" which God poured out on Sodom and Gomorrah (see Genesis 19:24) was but a foretaste of hell.

97

Strength of their dreams (verse 8). The godless men earned this name because they claimed to receive revelations in their sleep or, more likely, because their passions or lustful fantasies were out of touch with reality and morality.[3]

"The Lord rebuke you!" (verse 9). According to early church fathers, this quotation comes from the apocryphal book, *The Assumption of Moses*. Usage of material from such non-biblical sources does not suggest they are divinely inspired, only that the biblical author found secular sayings useful for illustrating or clarifying a point. Jude was not unique in this regard. Paul quoted the poets Aratus (see Acts 17:28), Menander (see 1 Corinthians 15:33), and Epimenides (see Titus 1:12).[4]

Way of Cain (verse 11). This could refer to selfishness and greed (see Genesis 4:3-4) or hatred and murder (see 1 John 3:12).

Balaam's error (verse 11). All-consuming greed. See notes on 2 Peter 2:14-16 (page 60).

Korah's rebellion (verse 11). This could refer to the rise of rebel leaders against God's ordained leaders in the church, as in Israel (see Numbers 16).

The archangel Michael (verse 9). This high-ranking angel appears throughout Scripture. Michael watched over Moses, arguing with the devil over Moses' body and leaving the final judgment of Satan to God.

He is also the "chief prince" who supported the prophet Daniel and protected Israel from Persia (see Daniel 10:13,21; 12:1).

Michael led the other angels in a heavenly battle against Satan and his fallen angels. Michael won and cast Satan and his angels from heaven to earth, where they led the world astray (see Revelation 12:7-12). Ultimately, Satan is completely defeated and an unnamed angel (often thought to be Michael) binds him for one thousand years and casts him into the lake of fire (see Revelation 20:1-10).

7. What do the apostates of Jude's day have in common with the three Old Testament examples of Cain, Balaam, and Korah (see verse 11)?

Cain_____

_____

_____

_____

Balaam _____

_____

_____

_____

Korah _____

_____

_____

_____

Who are these men? (12-16)

8. How are the apostates of Jude's day like each of the metaphors in verses 12-13?

blemishes at your love feasts

_____

_____

_____

_____

shepherds who feed only themselves

_____

_____

_____

_____

For Further Study: What is the point of the story of Michael disputing Satan with restraint and a rebuke from God, but not daring to "condemn him for slander"?

For Further Study: Many others brought division to the early church. Check out the super apostles (see 2 Corinthians 11), the dogs (see Philippians 3:2), and the worm-like household intruders (see 2 Timothy 3:6) that Paul had to contend with. Other unwelcome, ungodly, untrue prophets were deplored by Peter (see 2 Peter 2) and John (see 1 John 4:1; 2 John 7; 3 John 9).

clouds without rain

_____

_____

_____

_____

trees, without fruit and uprooted—twice dead

_____

_____

_____

_____

wild waves . . . foaming up their shame

_____

_____

_____

_____

wandering stars

_____

_____

_____

_____

Study Skill—Metaphors
A metaphor is a figure of speech used to shed new light on something by simply referring to it as something else—"All the world's a stage"—in order to imply a comparison between two (usually dissimilar) things. The reference is not intended to be taken literally, but to add new insight to the subject. The apostates are not really clouds; Peter is simply trying to tell us something about these men by using this image.

Blemishes at your love feasts (verse 12). The
Greek word *spiladees* (the plural form of *spi-
las*), is used here. But "hidden reefs" or *spilos*
in Greek better fits Peter's strong use of nature
imagery in verses 12-13. "Love feasts" refers to
the Lord's Supper. As hidden reefs are close to
shore and put incoming ships at peril, so these
apostates cause some to shipwreck in their
faith by their scandalous participation in the
sacrament.[5]

Wandering stars (verse 13). The Greek, *planeetai
asteeros*, suggests a pun on *planee* (translated
"error" or deception, of Balaam, verse 11).
Celestial bodies with irregular orbits will lead
astray anyone who tries to navigate by them.
"It is impossible to get spiritual direction from
these religious meteors, falling stars, and
comets, who blaze brightly for a moment, then
fizzle out into darkness like fireworks rockets."[6]

9. Jude quotes Enoch in verses 14-15. What is the
   point of Enoch's prophecy?

   _____

   _____

   _____

   _____

Enoch, the seventh from Adam (verse 14). This
is the Enoch in the line of Seth (see Genesis
5:18-24; 1 Chronicles 1:1-3), not the Enoch in
the line of Cain (see Genesis 4:17). The former
is purported to be the author of the apocryphal
book *1 Enoch*, which did not actually appear
until the first century BC. That Jude quotes
from the book of Enoch does not make it
inspired (see verse 9 and related note about *The
Assumption of Moses*). But neither does a work
have to be in the canon of Holy Scripture to
contain truth.

Ungodly . . . ungodliness . . . ungodly (verse 15). Jude's denunciation of these godless people and libertine false teachers (see verse 4) is made all the more scathing by the sheer repetition of this indictment.

10. Do you think the "ungodly" deny Christ and undermine the faith more by their beliefs (see verse 4), their behavior (see verses 15-16), or their influence on others (see verses 12-13,19)? Why?

_____

_____

_____

_____

_____

_____

Exhorting the believers (17-23)

11. a. What does Jude want his readers (and us) to remember?

_____

_____

_____

   b. What does he want us to do?

_____

_____

_____

_____

102

Remember what the apostles . . . foretold (verse
17). The presence of godless men should not
be a surprise, because Paul had warned of
"wolves" (Acts 20:29-30) and "worms"
(2 Timothy 3:1-9), even the "man of lawless-
ness" (2 Thessalonians 2:1-12). The Spirit
(see 1 Timothy 4:1) and Jesus Himself (see
Matthew 24:4-5,10-11; Mark 13:22) also warned
of false prophets and false messiahs.

People who divide you (verse 19). As divisive as
they were by their unbelief and scandalous
behavior, Gnostic heretics were also known to
divide people into two camps: (1) the spiritual
ones (Gnostics), and (2) the sensual or car-
nal ones (those for whom there is no hope).[7]
Jude counters that divisiveness with his plea
for building up, prayer, relying on the Spirit,
waiting, and showing mercy (see verses 20-23).

Praying in the Holy Spirit (verse 20). Prayer
should be in response to the prompting of the
Spirit, especially in our weakness or when we
are at a loss for words (see Romans 8:26-27;
Galatians 4:6; Ephesians 6:18). This phrase
does not imply "speaking in tongues," or a
special prayer language (see 1 Corinthians
12:10-11; 14:2,15).

Wait for the mercy . . . eternal life (verse 21).
Here, mercy offers the ultimate relief and unin-
terrupted fellowship that is ours when the Lord
returns for His own people.

Be merciful . . . show mercy (verses 22-23).
What we receive from the Lord Jesus is what
we are expected to share with others; otherwise, the quality of mercy is diminished, even
negated, as with the unmerciful servant (see
Matthew 18:21-35). Mercy shown to sinners
should be full of urgency and empathy, but also
mixed with fear, lest the lure of sin entrap the
mercy-giver.

Clothing stained by corrupted flesh (verse 23). Sin
contaminates everything and everyone it touches.

12. How have you benefited from the Lord's mercy?

_____

_____

_____

_____

_____

13. To whom is God calling you to show His mercy this week? (Refresh your memory by reviewing this checklist from Jude.)

☐ Doubters who may be under the influence of false teachers
☐ Family members who do not understand things of the Spirit
☐ Scoffers who follow their own ungodly desires
☐ Divisive people who may be wreaking havoc in your church
☐ Grumblers, faultfinders, braggarts, self-promoters
☐ Those who have slandered you or speak abusively about you
☐ Others who could still be snatched from the fires of hell
☐ Other: _____

_____

_____

_____

Benediction (24-25)

14. Meditate on Jude's famous benediction (see verses 24-25). What one key precept will you work through with God?

_____

_____

_____

_____

For the group

Warm-up. It's hard when we have a personality clash with someone. But much more than personality differences are at stake for Jude and his readers. His sense of betrayal, hurt, and anger comes from contending with apostates who espouse Christianity, but turn from that faith and seduce others. Jude confronts an apostasy that undermines grace, disdains authority, and appears beyond repentance and redemption.

Ask the group to focus on Jude's sense of betrayal, hurt, and anger. Ask one of two questions:

1. "Who is the most difficult person you've had to contend with (at work, in church, or on the home front), and with whom it is almost always a contest of wills and strength?" (Without naming names, how have you managed to do battle with this person?)
2. "Have you ever been on the receiving end of a sound rebuke (whether or not it was deserved)?" (What was that like?)

Outline of Jude

Purpose: To contend for the truth of the Christian faith against the sin and false teaching of heretics.

1-25	Warnings Against False Teachers
1-2	Jude identifies with Christ and greets fellow believers.
3-4	Jude clarifies his reason for writing.
5-7	Jude reminds readers that God has always judged false teachers, even fallen angels.
8-10	Jude asserts that dreamers who defame God will surely perish.
11	Jude condemns the way of Cain, Balaam, and Korah.
12-13	Jude reminds readers that an empty, shameless life of sin is short-lived.
14-16	Jude quotes Enoch who says that God will come to judge ungodly lifestyles.

17-19	Jude warns that scoffers of truth will try to divide the Church..
20-21	Jude encourages the believer to pray in the Spirit and "keep" in God's love.
22-23	Jude urges the believer to show mercy to sinners, but hate their sin.
24-25	Jude reminds readers that God keeps and presents as holy those who trust Him.

1. Donald Burdick and John Skilton, "1 & 2 Peter," *The NIV Study Bible*, ed. Kenneth Barker (Grand Rapids, MI: Zondervan, 1985), 1920.
2. Burdick and Skilton, 1920; also J. N. D. Kelly, *A Commentary on the Epistles of Peter and Jude* (Grand Rapids, MI: Baker, 1981), 252.
3. Burdick and Skilton, 1920.
4. Burdick and Skilton, 1920.
5. Kelly, 270–271.
6. William MacDonald, *II Peter and Jude: The Christian & Apostasy* (Wheaton, IL: Harold Shaw, 1972), 86.
7. Burdick and Skilton, 1921.

REVIEW

Reread all of 2 Peter and Jude. The material will be familiar to you by now, so you should be able to read quickly, looking for key words and phrases that tie the books together. Pray for a fresh perspective on what God is saying through these books.

1. In lesson 1, question 7, you said what you thought Peter's main purpose in writing this second letter was. After doing this study, how would you now summarize Peter's main goal?

   _____

   _____

   _____

   _____

   _____

   _____

   _____

   _____

2. What are the most important lessons you learned about each of the following?

salvation's security _____

_____

_____

_____

_____

the validity of Scripture _____

_____

_____

_____

_____

false teachers _____

_____

_____

_____

the end times _____

_____

_____

_____

_____

God's timing _____

_____

_____

_____

_____

perseverance _____

_____

_____

_____

other key lessons _____

_____

_____

_____

_____

_____

_____

3. What do you "already know" from 2 Peter that puts you in good stead to . . .

discern false prophets?_____

_____

_____

_____

_____

know the truth from God's Word?_____

_____

_____

_____

live in the hope of the Lord's return? _____

_____

_____

_____

_____

_____

survive the Lord's judgment to come? _____

_____

_____

_____

guard against falling?_____

_____

_____

_____

grow in grace? _____

_____

_____

_____

4. Have you noticed any areas (attitudes, opinions, thoughts, relationships with people, general behavior, and so on) in which you have changed as a result of studying 2 Peter and Jude? How have you changed?

_____

_____

_____

_____

_____

5. Look back through the study, noting places where you expressed a desire to make some personal application. Are you happy with your follow-through? Pray about any of those areas that you think you should continue to pursue. Write any notes here.

_____

_____

_____

_____

_____

For the group

After going over the questions in this review lesson, let anyone in the group ask any questions he or she may still have about 2 Peter or Jude. Allow others in the group to respond to the questions if they have any insights or answers. If questions remain unanswered, make plans for someone to check one of the sources in the Study Aids for insights that might help. The results can be shared at the next meeting.

At this point, you may want to evaluate how well your group functioned during your study of 2 Peter and Jude. Questions you might ask include:

- What did you learn about small-group study?
- What did members like best about group study? What could be improved?
- Were the needs of individual members met on a regular basis? (If not, what changes can be made in the group to rectify the situation for future meetings?)
- Was everyone able to share ideas?
- Was group prayer-time beneficial?
- What steps can you take to meet the current needs of your group members?
- What will the group do next?

STUDY AIDS

For further information on the material covered in this study, consider the following sources. They are available on the Internet (www.christianbook.com, www.amazon.com, and so on), or your local Christian bookstore should be able to order any of them if it does not carry them. Most seminary libraries have them, as well as many university and public libraries. If they are out of print, you might be able to find them online.

Commentaries on 2 Peter and Jude

Barclay, William. *The Letters of James and Peter* (Philadelphia: Westminster, 1976).
> This very accessible commentary is often used for devotional reading because of its fresh translation and homiletic interpretation. However, the introduction is challenging and outlines the scholarly debate over the authorship and dating issues surrounding 2 Peter.

Barclay, William. *The Letters of John and Jude* (Philadelphia: Westminster, 1976)
> Part of Barclay's *Daily Study Bible* series, this commentary brings out the response of the early church to those who tried to introduce heretical teachings and bad morals.

DeHaan, Richard. *Studies in Second Peter* (Wheaton, IL: Victor, 1977).
> The author is a popular Bible teacher and his focus is particularly helpful for those modern readers who question their faith. His contemporary application is outstanding and helpful for those wanting to discern truth from heresy.

Kelly, J. N. D. *A Commentary on the Epistles of Peter and Jude* (Grand Rapids, MI: Baker, 1981).
> This is a useful and detailed commentary for serious Bible students. Kelly offers his own English translation and explains its relation to the original Greek text. On controversial points, he brings conservative and

mainline scholarship together. He also offers word studies to help with the reader's study of 2 Peter and Jude.

MacDonald, William. *II Peter & Jude: The Christian and Apostasy* (Wheaton, IL: Harold Shaw, 1972).
   The author, a fine Bible teacher in England and Europe, offers his own unique, word-by-word outline of these two New Testament letters. He then offers application for contemporary Christian living.

Nieboer, J. *Practical Exposition of II Peter* (North East, PA: Our Daily Walk Publishers, 1952).
   This 192-page book is volume 22 in the New Testament for Spiritual Reading series, edited by John L. McKenzie and translated from German. This brief, but to the point commentary is ideal for devotional reading.

Historical sources

Bruce, F. F. *New Testament History* (New York: Doubleday, 1971).
   A readable history of Herodian kings, Roman governors, philosophical schools, Jewish sects, Jesus, the early Jerusalem church, Paul, and early Gentile Christianity. Well-documented with footnotes for the serious student, but the notes do not intrude.

Harrison, E. F. *Introduction to the New Testament* (Grand Rapids, MI: Eerdmans, 1971).
   History from Alexander the Great—who made Greek culture dominant in the biblical world—through philosophies, pagan and Jewish religion, Jesus' ministry and teaching, and the spread of Christianity. Very good maps and photographs of the land, art, and architecture of New Testament times.

Hiebert, D. Edmond. *An Introduction to the New Testament* (Chicago: Moody, 1977).
   A conservative, easily digested guide to the systematic interpretation of the New Testament. Books are treated in chronological order with emphasis on their eschatology, soteriology, Christology, or ecclesiology.

Histories, concordances, dictionaries, and handbooks

A **concordance** lists words of the Bible alphabetically along with each verse in which the word appears. It lets you do your own word studies. An *exhaustive* concordance lists every word used in a given translation, while an *abridged* or *complete* concordance omits either some words, some occurrences of the word, or both.
   Two of the three best exhaustive concordances are the venerable *Strong's Exhaustive Concordance* and *Young's Analytical Concordance to the Bible*.

Both are available based on the King James Version and the New American Standard Bible. *Strong's* has an index in which you can find out which Greek or Hebrew word is used in a given English verse (although its information is occasionally outdated). *Young's* breaks up each English word it translates. Neither concordance requires knowledge of the original languages.

Perhaps the best exhaustive concordance currently on the market is *The NIV Exhaustive Concordance*. It features a Hebrew-to-English and a Greek-to-English lexicon (based on the eclectic text underlying the NIV), which are also keyed to *Strong's* numbering system.

Among other good, less expensive concordances, *Cruden's Complete Concordance* is keyed to the King James and Revised Versions, the *NIV Complete Concordance* is keyed to the New International Version. These include all references to every word included, but they omit "minor" words. They also lack indexes to the original languages.

A **Bible dictionary** or **Bible encyclopedia** alphabetically lists articles about people, places, doctrines, important words, customs, and geography of the Bible.

The New Bible Dictionary, edited by J. D. Douglas, F. F. Bruce, J. I. Packer, N. Hillyer, D. Guthrie, A. R. Millard, and D. J. Wiseman (Tyndale, 1982) is more comprehensive than most dictionaries. Its 1,300 pages include quantities of information along with excellent maps, charts, diagrams, and an index for cross-referencing.

Unger's Bible Dictionary by Merrill F. Unger (Moody, 1979) is equally good and is available in an inexpensive paperback edition.

The Zondervan Pictorial Encyclopedia edited by Merrill C. Tenney (Zondervan, 1975, 1976) is excellent and exhaustive, and has been revised and updated. Its five 1,000-page volumes represent a significant financial investment, however, and all but very serious students may prefer to use it at a church, public college, or seminary library.

Unlike a Bible dictionary in the above sense, *Vine's Expository Dictionary of New Testament Words* by W. E. Vine (various publishers) alphabetically lists major words used in the King James Version and defines each New Testament Greek word that the KJV translates with its English word. Vine's also lists verse references where that Greek word appears, so you can do your own cross-references and word studies without knowing any Greek.

Vine's is a good, basic book for beginners, but it is much less complete than other Greek helps for English speakers. More serious students might prefer *The New International Dictionary of New Testament Theology*, edited by Colin Brown (Zondervan) or *The Theological Dictionary of the New Testament* by Gerhard Kittel and Gerhard Friedrich, abridged in one volume by Geoffrey W. Bromiley (Eerdmans).

A **Bible atlas** can be a great aid to understanding what is going on in a book of the Bible and how geography affected events. Here are a few good choices.

The Macmillan Atlas by Yohanan Aharoni and Michael Avi-Yonah (Macmillan, 1968, 1977) contains 264 maps, 89 photos, and 12 graphics. The many maps of individual events portray battles, movements of people, and changes of boundaries in detail.

The New Bible Atlas by J. J. Bimson and J. P. Kane (Tyndale, 1985) has 73 maps, 34 photos, and 34 graphics. Its evangelical perspective, concise and helpful text, and excellent research make it a very good choice, but its greatest strength lies in outstanding graphics, such as cross-sections of the Dead Sea.

The Bible Mapbook by Simon Jenkins (Lion, 1984) is much shorter and less expensive than most other atlases, so it offers a good first taste of the usefulness of maps. It contains 91 simple maps, very little text, and 20 graphics. Some of the graphics are computer-generated and intriguing.

The Moody Atlas of Bible Lands by Barry J. Beitzel (Moody, 1984), is scholarly, evangelical, and full of theological text, indexes, and references. This admirable reference work will be too deep and costly for some, but Beitzel shows vividly how God prepared the land of Israel perfectly for the acts of salvation He planned to accomplish in it.

A **handbook** of biblical customs can also be useful. Some good ones are *Today's Handbook of Bible Times and Customs* by William L. Coleman (Bethany, 1984) and the less detailed *Daily Life in Bible Times* (Nelson, 1982).

For small-group leaders

Barker, Steve, et al. *The Small Group Leader's Handbook* (Downer's Grove, IL: InterVarsity, 1982).

Written by an InterVarsity small group with college students primarily in mind. It includes information on small-group dynamics and how to lead in light of them, and many ideas for worship, building community, and outreach. It has a good chapter on doing inductive Bible study.

Griffin, Em. *Getting Together: A Guide for Good Groups* (Downer's Grove, IL: InterVarsity, 1982).

Applies to all kinds of groups, not just Bible studies. From his own experience, Griffin draws deep insights into why people join groups; how people relate to each other; and principles of leadership, decision making, and discussions. It is fun to read, but its 229 pages will take more time than the above book.

Hunt, Gladys. *You Can Start a Bible Study Group* (Wheaton, IL: Harold Shaw, 1984).

Builds on Hunt's thirty years of experience leading groups. This book is wonderfully focused on God's enabling. It is both clear and applicable for Bible study groups of all kinds.

McBride, Neal F. *How to Build a Small Groups Ministry* (Colorado Springs, CO: NavPress, 1994).

This hands-on .workbook for pastors and lay leaders includes everything you need to know to develop a plan that fits your unique church. Through basic principles, case studies, and worksheets, McBride leads you through twelve logical steps for organizing and administering a small-groups ministry.

McBride, Neal F. *How to Lead Small Groups* (Colorado Springs, CO: NavPress, 1990).

Covers leadership skills for all kinds of small groups—Bible study, fellowship, task, and support groups. Filled with step-by-step guidance and practical exercises to help you grasp the critical aspects of small-group leadership and dynamics.

Bible study methods

Braga, James. *How to Study the Bible* (Colorado Springs, CO: Multnomah, 1982).

Clear chapters on a variety of approaches to Bible study: synthetic, geographical, cultural, historical, doctrinal, practical, and so on. Designed to help the ordinary person without seminary training use these approaches.

Fee, Gordon, and Douglas Stuart. *How to Read the Bible for All Its Worth* (Grand Rapids, MI: Zondervan, 1982).

After explaining in general what interpretation and application are, Fee and Stuart offer chapters on interpreting and applying the different kinds of writing in the Bible: Epistles, Gospels, Old Testament Law, Old Testament narrative, the Prophets, Psalms, Wisdom, and Revelation. Fee and Stuart also suggest good commentaries on each biblical book. They write as evangelical scholars who personally recognize Scripture as God's Word for their daily lives.

Jensen, Irving L. *Independent Bible Study* (Chicago: Moody, 1963), and *Enjoy Your Bible* (Moody, 1962).

The former is a comprehensive introduction to the inductive Bible study method, especially the use of synthetic charts. The latter is a simpler introduction to the subject.

Wald, Oletta. *The Joy of Discovery in Bible Study* (Minneapolis, MN: Augsburg, 1975).

Wald focuses on issues such as how to observe all that is in a text, how to ask questions of a text, how to use grammar and passage structure to see the writer's point, and so on. Very helpful on these subjects.

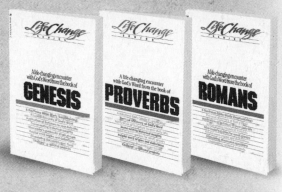

SUPPORT THE MINISTRY OF THE NAVIGATORS

The Navigators' calling is to advance the gospel of Jesus and His kingdom into the nations through spiritual generations of laborers living and discipling among the lost.

Navigators have invested their lives in people for more than 75 years, coming alongside them life on life to help them passionately know Christ and to make Him known.

The U.S. Navigators' ministry touches lives in varied settings, including college campuses, military bases, downtown offices, urban neighborhoods, prisons, and youth camps.

Dedicated to helping people navigate spiritually, The Navigators aims to make a permanent difference in the lives of people around the world. The Navigators helps its communities of friends to follow Christ passionately and equip them effectively to go out and do the same.

To learn more about donating to The Navigators' ministry,
go to **www.navigators.org/us/support**
or call toll-free at **1-866-568-7827**.